Toward a History of Needs

Toward a History of Needs

Ivan Illich

equinox

SHEFFIELD UK BRISTOL CT

Published by Equinox Publishing Ltd.

UK: Office 415, The Workstation, 15 Paternoster Row,
Sheffield, South Yorkshire S1 2BX

USA: ISD, 70 Enterprise Drive, Bristol, CT 06010

www.equinoxpub.com

First published by Pantheon Books, 1977.
Reprinted by Equinox Publishing Ltd 2026.

British Library Cataloguing-in-Publication Data

A catalogue record for this book is available from the British Library.

ISBN-13	978 1 80050 870 5	(hardback)
	978 1 80050 871 2	(paperback)
	978 1 80050 872 9	(ePDF)
	978 1 80050 949 8	(ePub)

Library of Congress Cataloging-in-Publication Data

Illich, Ivan D., 1926–
Toward a History of Needs.
CONTENTS: Useful unemployment and its professional enemies.—Outwitting developed nations.—In lieu of education.—Tantalizing needs. [etc.]
1. Social history—20th century—Addresses, essays, lectures. 2. Social problems—Addresses, essays, lectures. 3. Economic development—Social aspects—Addresses, essays, lectures. I. Title.
HN16.I36 1978 309.1'04 77–14050

Typeset by Isabelle Cedotti

Contents

Introduction

The five essays in this volume reflect a decade's thinking on the industrial mode of production. During this period, I have focused on the processes through which growing dependence on mass-produced goods and services gradually erodes the conditions necessary for a convivial life. In examining a distinct area of economic growth, each essay demonstrates a general rule: use-values are inevitably destroyed when the industrial mode of production achieves the predominance that I have termed "radical monopoly." These pieces describe how industrial growth produces the modernization of poverty.

Modernized poverty appears when the intensity of market dependence reaches a certain threshold. Subjectively, it is the experience of frustrating affluence which occurs in persons mutilated by their overwhelming reliance on the riches of industrial productivity. Simply, it deprives those affected by it of their freedom and power to act autonomously, to live creatively; it confines them to survival through being plugged into market relations. And precisely because this new impotence is so deeply experienced, it is with difficulty expressed. We are the witnesses of a barely perceptible transformation in ordinary language by which verbs that formerly designated satisfying actions are replaced by nouns that denote packages designed for passive consumption only: for example, "to learn" becomes "the acquisition of credits." A profound change in individual and social self-images is here reflected. And the layman is not the only one who has difficulty in accurately describing what he experiences. The professional economist is unable to recognize the poverty his conventional instruments fail to uncover.

Nevertheless, the new mutant of impoverishment continues to spread. The peculiarly modern inability to use personal endowments, communal life, and environmental resources in an autonomous way infects every aspect of life where a professionally engineered commodity has succeeded in replacing a culturally shaped use-value. The opportunity to experience personal and social satisfaction outside the market is thus destroyed. I am poor, for instance, when the use-value of my feet is lost because I live in Los Angeles or work on the thirty-fifth floor.

This new impotence-producing poverty must not be confused with the widening gap between the consumption of rich and poor in a world where basic needs are increasingly shaped by industrial commodities. That gap is the form traditional poverty assumes in an industrial society, and the conventional terms of class struggle appropriately reveal and reduce it. I further distinguish modernized poverty from the burdensome price exacted by the externalities which increased levels of production spew into the environment. It is clear that these kinds of pollution, stress, and taxation are unequally imposed. Correspondingly, defenses against such depredations are unequally distributed. But like the new gaps in access, such inequities in social costs are aspects of industrialized poverty for which economic indicators and objective verification can be found. Such is not true for the industrialized impotence which affects both rich and poor. Where this kind of poverty reigns, life without addictive access to commodities is rendered either impossible or criminal. Making do without consumption becomes impossible, not just for the average consumer but even for the poor. All forms of welfare, from affirmative action to environmental action, are of no help. The liberty to design and craft one's own distinctive dwelling is abolished in favor of the bureaucratic provision of standardized housing, as in the United States, Cuba, or Sweden. The organization of employment, skills, building resources, rules, and credit favor shelter as a commodity rather than as an activity. Whether the product is provided by an entrepreneur or an *apparatchik*, the effective result is the same: citizen impotence, our specifically modern experience of poverty.

Wherever the shadow of economic growth touches us, we are left useless unless employed on a job or engaged in consumption; the attempt to build a house or set a bone outside the control of certified specialists appears as anarchic conceit. We lose sight of our resources, lose control over the environmental conditions which make these resources applicable, lose the taste for self-reliance, for coping with challenges from without and anxiety from within. Take childbirth in Mexico today: delivery without professional care has become unthinkable for those women whose husbands are regularly employed and therefore have access to social services, no matter how marginal or tenuous. They move in circles where the production of babies faithfully reflects the patterns of industrial outputs. Yet their sisters in the slums of the poor or the villages of the isolated still feel quite competent in giving birth on their own mats, unaware that they face a modern indictment of criminal neglect toward their infants. But as professionally engineered delivery models reach these independent women, the desire, competence, and conditions for autonomous behavior are being destroyed.

For advanced industrial society, the modernization of poverty means that people are helpless to recognize evidence unless it has been certified by a professional, be he a television weather commentator or an educator; that organic discomfort becomes intolerably threatening unless it has been medicalized into dependence on a therapist; that neighbors and friends are lost unless vehicles bridge the separating distance (created by the vehicles in the first place). In short, most of the time we find ourselves out of touch with our world, out of sight of those for whom we work, out of tune with what we feel.

At the invitation of André Schiffrin, my United States publisher, I have selected five essays which review and develop my arguments on these themes. With their publication, I want to close ten years of teaching and writing about the counterproductive myth-making which is latent in all present-day industrial enterprises.

The first essay is a postscript to my book *Tools for Conviviality* (New York, 1973). It reflects the changes that have occurred during the past decade, both in economic reality and in my own perceptions of it. It assumes a rather large increase in the non-technical, ritual, and symbolic powers of our major technological and bureaucratic systems, and a corresponding decrease in their scientific, technical, and instrumental effectiveness. In 1968, it was still quite easy to dismiss organized lay resistance to professional dominance as nothing more than a throwback to romantic, obscurantist, or elitist fantasies. The grassroots, common-sense assessment of technological systems I then outlined seemed childish or retrograde to the political leaders of citizen activism, and to the "radical" professionals who laid claim to the tutorship of the poor by means of their special knowledge. The reorganization of industrial society around professionally defined needs, problems, and solutions was still the commonly accepted value implicit in ideological, political, and juridical systems otherwise clearly and sometimes violently opposed to one another.

Now, the picture has changed. Today, a hallmark of advanced and enlightened technical competence is a self-confident community, neighborhood, or group of citizens engaged in the systematic analysis and consequent ridicule of the "needs," "problems," and "solutions" defined for them by the agents of professional establishments. In the sixties, lay opposition to legislation based upon expert opinion still sounded like anti-scientific bigotry. Today, lay confidence in public policies based upon the expert's opinion is tenuous indeed. Thousands now reach their own judgments and, at great cost, engage in citizen action without any professional tutorship; they gain the scientific information they need through personal, independent effort. Sometimes risking limb, freedom, and respectability, they bear witness to a newly matured scientific attitude. They know, for example, that the quality and amount of technical evidence sufficiently conclusive to oppose atomic power plants, the multiplication of intensive-care units, compulsory education, fetal monitoring, psychosurgery, electroshock treatment, or genetic engineering is also simple and clear enough for the layman to grasp and utilize.

Ten years ago, compulsory schooling was still protected by powerful taboos. Today, its defenders are almost exclusively either teachers whose jobs depend upon it or Marxist ideologues who defend professional knowledge-holders in a shadow battle against the hip-bourgeoisie. Ten years ago, the myths about the effectiveness of modern medical institutions were still unquestioned. Most economics textbooks accepted the belief that adult life expectancy was increasing, that treatment for cancer postponed death, and that the availability of doctors resulted in higher infant-survival rates. Since then, people have "discovered" what vital statistics have always shown: that adult life expectancy has not changed in any socially significant way over the last few generations; that it is lower in most rich countries today than in our grandparents' time, and also lower there than in many poor nations. Ten years ago, universal access to post-secondary schooling, to adult education, to preventive medicine, to highways, to a wired global village, was still a prestigious goal. Today, the great myth-making rituals organized around education, transportation, health care, and urbanization have indeed been partly demystified. They have not yet, however, been disestablished.

The second essay is the text of a speech I delivered to the Canadian Foreign Policy Association in 1969. It is a critique of the *Pearson Report*, a document intended to conclude the first so-called "development decade" and open the second. Herein, I called attention to the exasperating impotence that is inflicted upon the poor in those countries which have benefited most from the importation of the public utilities in which the rich take pride.

The last three essays focus on the kind of social and political paralysis which cripples not just the poor but the vast majority in the industrialized nations. The production of modernized poverty in the shadow of economic expansion is described principally in the areas of transportation, education, and health care. It is from these sectors that I have learned much during this decade.

Shadow prices and increased consumption gaps are important aspects of the new poverty, but my principal interest is directed toward a different concomitant of modernization: the process by which autonomy is undermined, satisfaction dulled, experience flattened out, and needs frustrated for nearly everyone. For example, I have examined the society-wide obstacles to mutual presence which are necessary side effects of energy-intensive transportation. I have wanted to define the power limits of motors equitably used to increase people's access to one another. I recognized, of course, that high speeds inevitably impose a skewed distribution of harriedness, noise, pollution, and enjoyment of privilege. But my emphasis is other than this. My arguments are focused on the negative internalities of modernity-time-consuming acceleration, sick-making health care, stupefying education. The unequal distribution of the ersatz benefits, or the unequal imposition of their negative externalities, are corollaries to my basic argument. In these essays, I am interested in the direct and specific effects of modernized poverty, in human tolerance for such effects, and in the possibility of escaping the new misery.

During these last years, I have found it necessary to examine again and again the correlation between the nature of tools and the meaning of justice that prevails in the society that uses them. I have had to observe the decline of freedom in societies where rights are shaped by expertise. I have had to weigh the trade-offs between new tools that enhance the production of commodities and those equally modern ones that permit the generation of values in use; between rights to mass-produced commodities and the level of liberty that permits satisfying and creative personal expression; between paid employment and useful unemployment. And in each dimension of the trade-off between heteronomous management and autonomous action, I find that the language that would permit us to insist on the latter must be recovered with difficulty. I am, like those I seek as my readers, so profoundly committed to a radically equitable access to goods, rights, and jobs that I find it almost unnecessary to insist on our struggle for this side of justice. I find it much more important, and difficult, to deal with its complement: the politics of conviviality. I use this term in the technical sense I gave to it in *Tools for Conviviality*: to designate the struggle for an equitable distribution of the liberty to generate use-values and for the instrumentation of this liberty through the assignment of an absolute priority to the production of those industrial and professional commodities that confer on the least advantaged the greatest power to generate values in use.

New, convivial politics are based on the insight that in a modern society, both wealth and jobs can be equitably shared and enjoyed in liberty only when both are limited by a political process. Excessive forms of wealth and prolonged formal employment, no matter how well distributed, destroy the social, cultural, and environmental conditions for equal productive freedom. Bits and watts—which here stand for units of information and of energy, respectively—when packaged into any mass-produced commodity in amounts that pass a threshold, inevitably constitute impoverishing wealth. Such wealth is either too rare to be shared or it is destructive of the freedom and liberty of the weakest. With each of these five essays, I have attempted to make a contribution to the political process by which the socially critical thresholds of enrichment are recognized by citizens and translated into society-wide ceilings or limits.

1. Useful Unemployment and its Professional Enemies

This essay on trade-offs between commodities and use-values in a modern society was written in 1977 and is published here for the first time. John McKnight and Lee Hoinacki have helped me to clarify my thought. I am also indebted here to the work of William Leiss, who, in The Limits to Satisfaction *(Toronto, 1976), deals with the correlation of modern needs and commodities.*

Fifty years ago, most of the words an American heard were personally spoken to him as an individual, or to somebody standing nearby. Only occasionally did words reach him as an undifferentiated member of a crowd—in the classroom or in church, at a rally or a circus. Words were mostly like handwritten, sealed letters, and not like the junk that now pollutes our mails. Today, words that are directed to one person's attention have become rare. Engineered staples of images, ideas, feelings, and opinions, packaged and delivered through the media, assault our sensibilities with round-the-clock regularity. Two points now become evident: (1) what is occurring with language fits the pattern of an increasingly wide range of need-satisfaction relationships; and (2) this replacement of convivial means by manipulative industrial ware is truly universal, and is relentlessly making the New York teacher, the Chinese commune member, the Bantu schoolboy, and the Brazilian sergeant alike. In this essay, a postscript to *Tools for Conviviality*, I shall do three things: (1) describe the character of a commodity/market-intensive society in which the very abundance of commodities paralyzes the autonomous creation of use-values; (2) insist on the hidden role that professions play in such a society by shaping its needs; and (3) expose some illusions and propose some strategies for breaking the professional power that perpetuates market dependence.

Disabling Market Intensity

Crisis has come to mean that moment when doctors, diplomats, bankers, and assorted social engineers take over and liberties are suspended. Like patients, nations go on the critical list. *Crisis*, the Greek term that has designated "choice" or "turning point" in all modern languages, now means "driver, step on the gas." Crisis now evokes an ominous but tractable threat against which money, manpower, and management can be rallied. Intensive care for the dying, bureaucratic tutelage for the victim of discrimination, fission for the energy glutton, are typical responses. Crisis, understood in this way, is always good for executives and commissars, especially those scavengers who live on the side effects of yesterday's growth: educators who live on society's alienation, doctors who prosper on the work and leisure that have destroyed health, politicians who thrive on the distribution of welfare which, in the first instance, was financed by those assisted. Crisis, understood as a call for acceleration, not only puts more power under the control of the driver, while squeezing the passengers more tightly into their safety belts; it also justifies the depredation of space, time, and resources for the sake of motorized wheels, and it does so to the detriment of people who want to use their feet.

But crisis need not have this meaning. It need not imply a headlong rush for the escalation of management. Instead, it can mean the instant of choice, that marvelous moment when people suddenly become aware of their self-imposed cages and of the possibility of a different life. And this is the crisis that, as choice, confronts both the United States and the world today.

A World-Wide Choice

In only a few decades, the world has become an amalgam. Human responses to everyday occurrences have been standardized. Though languages and gods still appear to be different, people daily join the stupendous majority who march to the beat of the very same megamachine. The light switch by the door has replaced the dozens of ways in which fires, candles, and lanterns were formerly kindled. In ten years, the number of switch-users in the world has tripled; flush and paper have become essential conditions for the relief of the bowels. Light that does not flow from high-voltage networks and hygiene without tissue paper spell poverty for ever more people. Expectations grow, while hopeful trust in one's own competence and the concern for others rapidly decline.

The now soporific, now raucous intrusion of the media reaches deeply into the commune, the village, the corporation, the school. The sounds made by the editors and announcers of programmed texts daily pervert the words of a spoken language into building blocks for packaged messages. Today, one must be either isolated and cut off or a carefully guarded, affluent dropout to allow one's children to play in an environment where they listen to people rather than to stars, speakers, or instructors. All over the world, one can see the rapid encroachment of the disciplined acquiescence that characterizes the audience, the client, the customer. The standardization of human action grows apace.

It now becomes clear that most of the world's communities are facing exactly the same critical issue: people must either remain ciphers in the conditioned crowd that surges toward greater dependence (thus necessitating savage battles for a share of the drugs to feed their habit), or they must find the courage that alone saves in a panic: the courage to stand still and look around for another way out than the obvious marked exit. But many, when told that Bolivians, Canadians, and Hungarians all face the same fundamental choice, are not simply annoyed but deeply offended. The idea appears not only foolish, but shocking. They fail to detect the sameness in the new bitter degradation that underlies the hunger of the Indian in the Altiplano, the neurosis of the worker in Amsterdam, and the cynical corruption of the bureaucrat in Warsaw.

Toward a Culture for Staples

Development has had the same effect in all societies: everyone has been enmeshed in a new web of dependence on commodities that flow out of the same kind of machines, factories, clinics, television studios, think tanks. To satisfy this dependence, more of the same must be produced: standardized, engineered goods, designed for the future consumer who will be trained by the engineer's agent to need what he or she is offered. These products, be they tangible goods or intangible services, constitute the industrial staple. Their imputed monetary value as a commodity is determined by state and market in varying proportions. Thus, different cultures become insipid residues of traditional styles of action, washed up in one world-wide wasteland: an arid terrain devastated by the machinery needed to produce and consume. On the banks of the Seine and those of the Niger, people have unlearned how to milk because the white stuff now comes from the grocer. (Thanks to more richly endowed consumer protection, it is less poisonous in France than in Mali.) True, more babies get cow's milk, but the breasts of both rich and poor dry up. The addicted consumer is born when the baby cries for the bottle; when the organism is trained to reach for milk from the grocer and to turn away from the breast that thus defaults. Autonomous and creative human action, required to make man's universe bloom, atrophies. Roofs of shingle or thatch, tile or slate, are displaced by concrete for the few and corrugated plastic for the many. Neither jungles, swamps, nor ideological biases have prevented the poor and the socialist from rushing onto the highways of the rich, the roads leading them into the world where economists replace priests. The mint stamps out all local treasures and idols. Money devalues what it cannot measure. The crisis, then, is the same for all: the choice of more or less dependence upon industrial commodities. *More* will mean the rapid and complete destruction of cultures which are programs for satisfying subsistence activities. *Less* will mean the variegated flowering of use-values in modern cultures of intense activity. For both rich and poor, the choice is essentially the same, although hard to imagine for those already accustomed to living inside the supermarket—a structure different only in name from a ward for idiots.

Present-day industrial society organizes life around commodities. Our market-intensive societies measure material progress by the increase in the volume and variety of commodities produced. And, taking our cue from this sector, we measure social progress by the distribution of access to these commodities. Economics has been developed as propaganda for the takeover by large-scale commodity producers. Socialism has been debased to a struggle against handicapped distribution, and welfare economics has identified the public good with opulence—the humiliating opulence of the poor in United States hospitals, jails, or asylums.

By disregarding all trade-offs to which no price tag is attached, industrial society has created an urban landscape that is unfit for people unless they devour each day their own weight in metals and fuels, a world in which the constant need for protection against the unwanted results of more things and more commands has generated new depths of discrimination, impotence, and frustration. The establishment-orientated ecological movement has so far further strengthened this trend: it has concentrated attention on faulty industrial technology and, at best, on the exploitation of industrial production by private owners. It has questioned the depletion of natural resources, the inconvenience of pollution, and net transfers of power. But even when price tags are attached that reflect the environmental impact, the disvalue of nuisance, or the cost of polarization, we still do not see clearly that the division of labor, the multiplication of commodities, and dependence on them have forcibly substituted standardized packages for almost everything people formerly did or made on their own.

For two decades now, about fifty languages have died each year; half of those still spoken in 1950 survive only as subjects for doctoral theses. And what distinct languages do remain to witness the incomparably different ways of seeing, using, and enjoying the world now sound more and more alike. Consciousness is everywhere colonized by imported labels. Yet even those who do worry about the loss of cultural and genetic variety, or about the multiplication of long-impact isotopes, do not advert to the irreversible depletion of skills, stories, and senses of form. And this progressive substitution of industrial goods and services for useful but nonmarketable values has been the shared goal of political factions and regimes otherwise violently opposed to one another.

In this way, ever larger pieces of our lives are so transformed that life itself comes to depend almost exclusively on the consumption of commodities sold on the world market. The United States corrupts its farmers to provide grain to a regime which increasingly stakes its legitimacy on the ability to deliver even more grain. Of course, the two regimes allocate resources by different methods: here, by the wisdom of pricing; there, by the wisdom of planners. But the political opposition between proponents of alternate methods of allocation only masks the similar ruthless disregard of personal dignity and freedom by all factions and parties.

Energy policy is a good example of the profound identity in the world-views of the self-styled socialist and the so-called "capitalist" supporters of the industrial system. Possibly excluding such places as Cambodia, about which I am uninformed, no governing elite nor any socialist opposition can conceive of a desirable future that would be based on per capita energy consumption of a magnitude inferior to that which now prevails in Europe. All existing political parties stress the need for energy-intensive production—albeit with Chinese discipline—while failing to comprehend that the corresponding society will further deny people the free use of their limbs. Here sedans and there buses push bicycles off the road. All governments stress an employment-intensive force of production, but are unwilling to recognize that jobs can also destroy the use-value of free time. They all stress a more objective and complete professional definition of people's needs, but are insensitive to the consequent expropriation of life.

In the late Middle Ages, the stupefying simplicity of the heliocentric model was used as an argument to discredit the new astronomy. Its elegance was interpreted as naivete. In our days, use-value-centered theories that analyze the social costs generated by established economics are certainly not rare. Such theories are being proposed by dozens of outsiders, who often identify them with radical technology, ecology, community life-styles, smallness, or beauty. As an excuse to avoid looking at these theories, the frequent failure of their proponents' experiments in personal living is held against them, and magnified. Just as the legendary inquisitor refused to look through Galileo's telescope, so most modern economists refuse to look at an analysis that might displace the conventional center of their economic system. The new analytical systems would force us to recognize the obvious: that the generation of nonmarketable use-values must inevitably occupy the center of any culture that provides a program for satisfactory life to a majority of its members. Cultures are programs for activities, not for firms. Industrial society destroys this center by polluting it with the measured output of corporations, public or private, degrading what people do or make on their own. As a consequence, societies have been transformed into huge zero-sum games, monolithic delivery systems in which every gain for one turns into a loss or burden for another, while true satisfaction is denied to both.

On the way, innumerable sets of infrastructures in which

people coped, played, ate, made friends, and made love have been destroyed. A couple of so-called "development decades" have sufficed to dismantle traditional patterns of culture, from Manchuria to Montenegro. Prior to these years, such patterns permitted people to satisfy most of their needs in a subsistence mode. After these years, plastic had replaced pottery, carbonated beverages replaced water, Valium replaced chamomile tea, and records replaced guitars. All through history, the best measure for bad times was the percentage of food eaten that had to be purchased. In good times, most families got most of their nutrition from what they grew or acquired in a network of gift relationships. Until late in the eighteenth century, more than ninety-nine percent of the world's food was produced inside the horizon that the consumer could see from the church steeple or minaret. Laws that tried to control the number of chickens and pigs within the city walls suggest that, except for a few large urban areas, more than half of all food eaten was also cultivated within the city. Before World War II, less than four percent of all food eaten was transported into the region from abroad, and these imports were largely confined to the eleven cities which then contained more than two million inhabitants. Today, forty percent of all people survive only because they have access to interregional markets. A future in which the world market of capital and goods would be severely reduced is as much taboo today as a world in which active people would use modern convivial tools to create an abundance of use-values that would liberate them from consumption. One can see in this pattern a reflection of the belief that useful activities by which people both express and satisfy their needs can be replaced indefinitely by standardized goods or services.

The Modernization of Poverty

Beyond a certain threshold, the multiplication of commodities induces impotence, the incapacity to grow food, to sing, or to build. The toil and pleasure of the human condition become a faddish privilege restricted to some of the rich. When Kennedy launched the Alliance for Progress, Acatzingo, like most Mexican villages of its size, had four groups of musicians who played for a drink and served the population of eight hundred. Today, records and radios, hooked up to loudspeakers, drown out local talent. Occasionally, in an act of nostalgia, a collection is taken up to bring a band of dropouts from the university to sing the old songs for some special holiday. On the day Venezuela legislated the right of each citizen to "housing," conceived of as a commodity, three-quarters of all families found that their self-built dwellings were thereby degraded to the status of hovels. Furthermore—and this is the rub—self-building was now prejudiced. No house could be legally started without the submission of an approved architect's plan. The useful refuse and junk of Caracas, until then re-employed as excellent building materials, now created a problem of solid-waste disposal. The man who produces his own "housing" is looked down upon as a deviant who refuses to cooperate with the local pressure group for the delivery of mass-produced housing units. Also, innumerable regulations have appeared which brand his ingenuity as illegal or even criminal. This example illustrates how the poor are the first to suffer when a new kind of commodity castrates one of the traditional subsistence crafts. The useful unemployment of the jobless poor is sacrificed to the expansion of the labor market. "Housing," as a self-chosen activity, just like any other freedom for useful employment of time off the job, becomes the privilege of some deviant, often the idle rich.

An addiction to paralyzing affluence, once it becomes ingrained in a culture, generates "modernized poverty." This is a form of disvalue necessarily associated with the proliferation of commodities. This rising disutility of industrial mass products has escaped the attention of economists because it is not accessible to their measurements, and of social services because it cannot be "operationalized." Economists have no effective means of including in their calculations the society-wide loss of a kind of satisfaction that has no market equivalent. Thus, one could today define economists as members of a fraternity which only accepts people who, in the pursuit of their professional work, can practice a trained social blindness toward the most fundamental trade-off in contemporary systems, both East and West: the decline in the individual-personal ability to do or make, which is the price of every additional degree of commodity affluence.

The existence and nature of modernized poverty remained hidden, even in ordinary conversation, as long as it primarily affected the poor. As development, or modernization, reached the poor—those who until then had been able to survive in spite of being excluded from the market economy—they were systematically compelled to survive by buying into a purchasing system which, for them, always and necessarily meant getting the dregs of the market. Indians in Oaxaca who formerly had no access to schools are now drafted into school to "earn" certificates that measure precisely their inferiority relative to the urban population. Furthermore—and this again is the rub—without this piece of paper they can no longer enter even the building trades. The modernization of "needs" always adds new discrimination to poverty.

Modernized poverty has now become the common experience of all except those who are so rich that they can drop out in luxury. As one facet of life after another becomes dependent on engineered supplies, few of us escape the recurrent experience of impotence. The average United States consumer is bombarded by a hundred advertisements per day, and reacts to many of them—more often than not—in a negative way. Even well-heeled shoppers acquire, with each new commodity, a fresh experience of disutility. They suspect they have purchased something of doubtful value, perhaps soon to become useless or even dangerous, and something that calls for an array of even more expensive complements. Affluent shoppers organize: they usually begin with demands for quality control and not infrequently generate consumer resistance. Across the tracks, slum neighborhoods "unplug" themselves from service and "care," from social work in South Chicago and from textbooks in Kentucky. Rich and poor are almost ready to recognize clearly a new form of frustrating wealth in the further expansion of a market-intensive culture. Also, the affluent come to sense their own plight as it is mirrored in the poor, though for the moment this intimation has not developed beyond a kind of romanticism.

The ideology that identifies progress with affluence is

not restricted to the rich countries. The same ideology degrades nonmarketable activities even in areas where, until recently, most needs were still met through a subsistence mode of life. For example, the Chinese—drawing inspiration from their own tradition—seemed willing and able to redefine technical progress, to opt for the bicycle over the jet plane. They seemed to stress local self-determination as a goal of inventive people rather than as a means for national defense. But by 1977, their propaganda was glorying in China's industrial capacity to deliver more health care, education, housing, and general welfare—at a lower cost. Merely tactical functions are provisionally assigned to the herbs in the bag of the barefoot doctor, and to labor-intensive production methods. Here, as in other areas of the world, the heteronomous—that is, other-directed—production of goods, standardized for categories of anonymous consumers, fosters unrealistic and ultimately frustrating expectations. Furthermore, the process inevitably corrupts the trust of people in their own and their neighbors' ever surprising autonomous competences. China simply represents the latest example of the particular Western version of modernization through intensive market dependence, seizing a traditional society as no cargo cult did even at its most irrational extreme.

The History of Needs

In both traditional and modern societies, an important change has occurred in a very short period: the means for the satisfaction of needs have been radically altered. The motor has sapped the muscle; instruction has deadened self-confident curiosity. As a consequence, both needs and wants have acquired a character for which there is no historical precedent. For the first time, needs have become almost exclusively coterminous with commodities. As long as most people walked wherever they wanted to go, they felt restrained mainly when their *freedom* was restricted. Now that they depend on transportation in order to move, they claim not a freedom but a *right* to passenger miles. And, as ever more vehicles provide ever more people with such "rights," the freedom to walk is degraded and eclipsed by the provision of these rights. For most people, wants follow suit. They cannot even imagine liberation from universal passengerhood—that is, the liberty of modern man in a modern world to move on his own.

This situation, by now a rigid interdependence of needs and market, is legitimated through appeal to the expertise of an elite whose knowledge, by its very nature, cannot be shared. Economists of rightist as well as leftist persuasion vouch to the public that an increase in jobs depends on more energy; educators persuade the public that law, order, and productivity depend on more instruction; gynecologists claim that the quality of infant life depends on their involvement in childbirth. Therefore, the near-universal extension of market intensity in the world's economies cannot be effectively questioned as long as the immunity of the elites that legitimate the nexus between commodity and satisfaction has not been destroyed. The point is well illustrated by a woman who told me about the birth of her third child. Having borne two children, she felt both competent and experienced. She was in the hospital and felt the child coming. She called the nurse, who, instead of helping, rushed for a sterile towel to press the baby's head back into the womb and ordered the mother to stop pushing because "Dr. Levy has not yet arrived."

But this is the moment for public decision, for political action instead of professional management. Modern societies, rich or poor, can move in either of two opposite directions. They can produce a new bill of goods—albeit safer, less wasteful, more easily shared—and thereby further intensify their dependence on consumer staples. Or, they can take a totally new approach to the interrelationship between needs and satisfactions. In other words, societies can either retain their market-intensive economies, changing only the design of the output, or they can reduce their dependence on commodities. The latter alternative entails the adventure of imagining and constructing new frameworks in which individuals and communities can develop a new kind of modern tool kit. This would be organized so as to permit people to shape and satisfy an expanding proportion of their needs directly and personally.

The first direction represents a continuing identification of technical progress with the multiplication of commodities. The bureaucratic managers of egalitarian persuasion and the technocrats of welfare would converge in a call for austerity: to shift from goods, such as jets, that obviously cannot be shared, to so-called "social" equipment like buses; to distribute more equitably the decreasing hours of employment available and ruthlessly limit the typical work week to about twenty hours on the job; to draft the new resource of unemployed life-time into retraining or voluntary service on the model of Mao, Castro, or Kennedy. This new stage of industrial society, though socialist, effective, and rational, would simply usher in a new state of the culture that downgraded the satisfaction of wants into the repetitive relief of imputed needs through engineered staples. At its best, this alternative would produce goods and services in smaller quantities, distribute them more equitably, and foster less envy. The symbolic participation of people in deciding what ought to be made might be transferred from a buck in the market to a gawk in the political assembly. The environmental impact of production could be softened. Among commodities, services, especially the various forms of social control, would certainly grow much faster than the manufacture of goods. Huge sums are already being spent on the oracle industry so that government prophets can spew out "alternative" scenarios designed to shore up this first choice. Interestingly, many of them have already reached the conclusion that the cost of the social controls necessary to enforce austerity in an ecologically feasible but still industry-centered society would be intolerable.

The second choice would bring down the curtain on absolute market dominance and foster an ethic of austerity for the sake of widespread satisfying action. If, in the first alternative, austerity would mean the individual's acceptance of managerial *ukases* for the sake of increased institutional productivity, austerity in the second alternative would mean that social virtue by which people recognize and decide limits on the maximum amount of instrumented power that anyone may claim, both for his own satisfaction and in the service of others. This convivial austerity inspires a society to protect personal use-value against disabling enrichment. Under such protection against disabling affluence, many distinct cultures would arise, each modern and each emphasizing the dispersed use of modern tools. Convivial austerity so limits the use of any tool that tool ownership would lose much of its present power. If bicycles are owned here by the commune, there by the rider, nothing is changed about the essentially convivial nature of the bicycle as a tool. Such commodities would still be produced in large measure by industrial methods, but they would be seen and evaluated differently. Now, commodities are viewed mostly as staples that directly feed the needs shaped by their designers. In the second option, they would be valued either as raw materials or as tools that permitted people to generate use-values in maintaining the subsistence of their respective communities. But this choice depends, of course, on a Copernican revolution in our perception of values. At present, we see consumer goods and professional services at the center of our economic system, and specialists relate our needs exclusively to this center. In contrast, the social inversion contemplated here would assign to the center use-values created and personally fostered by people themselves. It is true that people have recently lost the confidence to shape their own desires. The world-wide discrimination against the autodidact has vitiated many people's confidence in determining their own goals and needs. But the same discrimination has also resulted in a multiplicity of growing minorities who are infuriated by this insidious dispossession.

Disabling Professions

These minorities already see that they—and all autochthonous cultural life—are threatened by megatools which systematically expropriate the environmental conditions that foster individual and group autonomy. And so they quietly determine to fight for the usefulness of their bodies, memories, and skills. Because the rapidly increasing multiplication of imputed needs generates ever new kinds of dependence and ever new categories of modernized poverty, present-day industrial societies take on the character of interdependent conglomerates of bureaucratically stigmatized majorities. Among this great mass of citizens who are crippled by transport, rendered sleepless by schedules, poisoned by hormone therapy, silenced by loudspeakers, sickened by food, a few form minorities of organized and active citizens. Now, these are barely beginning to grow and coalesce for public dissidence. Subjectively, these groups are ready to end an age. But to be dispatched, an age needs a name that sticks. I propose to call the mid-twentieth century the Age of Disabling Professions. I choose this designation because it commits those who use it. It exposes the antisocial functions performed by the least challenged providers—educators, physicians, social workers, and scientists. Simultaneously, it indicts the complacency of citizens who have submitted themselves to multifaceted bondage as clients. To speak about the power of disabling professions shames their victims into recognizing the conspiracy of the lifelong student, gynecological case, or consumer, each with his or her manager. By describing the sixties as an apogee of the problem-solver, one immediately exposes both the inflated conceit of our academic elites and the greedy gullibility of their victims.

But this focus on the makers of the social imagination and the cultural values does more than expose and denounce; by designating the last twenty-five years as the Age of Dominant Professions, one also proposes a strategy. One sees the necessity of going beyond the expert redistribution of wasteful, irrational, and paralyzing commodities, the hallmark of Radical Professionalism, the conventional wisdom of today's good guys. The strategy demands nothing less than the unmasking of the professional ethos. The credibility of the professional expert, be he scientist, therapist, or executive, is the Achilles' heel of the industrial system. Therefore, only those citizen initiatives and radical technologies that directly challenge the insinuating dominance of disabling professions open the way to freedom for nonhierarchical, community-based competence. The waning of the current professional ethos is a necessary condition for the emergence of a new relationship between needs, contemporary tools, and personal satisfaction. The first step toward this emergence is a skeptical and non-deferential posture of the citizen toward the professional expert. Social reconstruction begins with a doubt raised among citizens.

When I propose the analysis of professional power as the key to social reconstruction, I am usually told that it is a dangerous error to select this phenomenon as the crux for recovery from the industrial system. Does not the shape of the educational, medical, and planning establishments actually reflect the distribution of power and privilege of a capitalist elite? Is it not irresponsible to undermine the trust of the man in the street in his scientifically trained teacher, physician, or economist precisely at the moment when the poor need these trained protectors to gain access to classroom, clinic, and expert assistance? Ought not the indictment of the industrial system expose the income of stockholders in drug firms or the perquisites of power-brokers who belong to the new elites? Why spoil the mutual dependence of clients and professional providers, especially when increasingly—as in Cuba and the United States—both tend to come from the same social class? Is it not perverse to denigrate the very people who have painfully acquired the knowledge to recognize and service our needs for welfare? In fact, should not the radically socialist professional leaders be singled out as those most apt for the ongoing societal task of defining and meeting people's "real" needs in an egalitarian society?

The arguments implicit in these questions are frequently advanced to disrupt and discredit public analysis of the disabling effects of industrial welfare systems which focus on services. Such effects are essentially identical and clearly inevitable, no matter what the political flag under which they are imposed. They incapacitate people's autonomy by forcing them—via legal, environmental, and social changes—to become consumers of care. These rhetorical questions represent a frantic defense of privilege on the part of those elites who might lose income but would certainly gain status and power if, in a new form of market-intensive economy, dependence on their services were rendered more equitable.

A further objection to the critique of professional power drives out the devil with Beelzebub. This objection singles out as the key target for analysis the defense conglomerates seemingly at the center of each bureaucratic-industrial society. The developed argument then posits the security forces as the motor behind the contemporary universal regimentation into market-dependent discipline. It identifies as the principal need-makers the armed bureaucracies that have come into being since, under Louis XIV, Richelieu established the first professional police—that is, the professional agencies that are now in charge of weaponry, intelligence, and propaganda. Since Hiroshima, these so-called "services" appear to be the determinants for research, design production, and employment. They rest upon civilian foundations, such as schooling for discipline, consumer training for the enjoyment of waste, habituation to violent speeds, medical engineering for life in a world-wide shelter, and standardized dependence on rations dispensed by benevolent quartermasters. This line of thought sees state security as the generator of a society's production patterns, and views the civilian economy as, to a large extent, either the military's spin-off or its prerequisite.

If an argument constructed around these notions were valid, how could such a society forgo atomic power, no matter how poisonous, oppressive, or counterproductive a further energy glut might be? How could a defense-ridden state be expected to tolerate the organization of disaffected citizen groups who unplug their neighborhoods from consumption to claim the liberty of small-scale use-value-intensive production that happens in an atmosphere of satisfying and joyful austerity? Would not a militarized society soon have to move against need-deserters, brand them as traitors, and, if possible, expose them not just to scorn but to ridicule? Would not a defense-driven society have to stamp out those examples that would lead to nonviolent modernity, just at the time when public policy calls for a decentralization of commodity production reminiscent of Mao, and for more rational, equitable, and professionally supervised consumption?

This argument pays undue credit to the military as the source of violence in an industrial state. The assumption that military requirements are to blame for the aggressiveness and destructiveness of advanced industrial society must be exposed as an illusion. No doubt, if it were true that the military had somehow usurped the industrial system, if it had wrenched the various spheres of social endeavor and action away from civilian control, then the present state of militarized politics would have reached a point of no return—at least, of no potential for civilian reform. This is, in fact, the argument made by the brightest of Brazil's military leaders, who see the armed forces as the only legitimate tutor of peaceful industrial pursuit during the rest of this century.

But this is simply not so. The modern industrial state is not a product of the army. Rather, its army is one of the symptoms of its total and consistent orientation. True, the present industrial mode of organization can be traced to military antecedents in Napoleonic times. True, the compulsory education of peasant boys in the 1830s, the universal health care for the industrial proletariat in the 1850s, the growing communications networks in the 1860s, as well as most forms of industrial standardization, are all strategies first introduced into modern societies as military requirements and only later understood as dignified forms of peaceful, civilian progress. But the fact that systems of health, education, and welfare needed a military rationale to be enacted into law does not mean that they were not thoroughly consistent with the basic thrust of industrial development, which, in fact, was never nonviolent, peaceful, or respectful of people.

Today, this insight is easier to gain. First, because since Polaris it is no longer possible to distinguish between wartime and peacetime armies, and second, because since the war on poverty, peace is on the warpath. Today, industrial societies are constantly and totally mobilized; they are organized for constant public emergencies; they are shot through with variegated strategies in all sectors; the battlefields of health, education, welfare, and affirmative equality are strewn with victims and covered with ruins; citizens' liberties are continually suspended for campaigns against ever newly discovered evils; each year new frontier-dwellers are discovered who must be protected against or cured of some new disease, some previously unknown ignorance. The basic needs that are shaped and imputed by all professional agencies are needs for defense against evils.

Today's professors and social scientists who seek to blame the military for the destructiveness of commodity-intensive societies are people who, in a very clumsy way, are attempting to arrest the erosion of their own legitimacy. They claim that the military pushes the industrial system into its frustrating and destructive state, thereby distracting attention from the profoundly destructive nature of a market-intensive society which drives its citizens into today's wars. Both those who seek to protect professional autonomy against citizen maturity and those who wish to portray the professional as victim of the militarized state will be answered by a choice: the direction in which free citizens wish to go to supersede the world-wide crisis.

The Waning of the Professional Age

The illusions that permitted the installation of professions as arbiters of needs are now increasingly visible to common sense. Procedures in the service sector are often understood for what they are—Linus blankets, or rituals, that hide from the provider-consumer caboodle the disparity and antipathy between the ideal for the sake of which the service is rendered and the reality that the service creates. Schools that promise equal enlightenment generate unequally degrading meritocracy and lifelong dependence on further tutorship; vehicles compel everyone to a flight forward. But the public has not yet clarified the choices. Projects under professional leadership could result in compulsory political creeds (with their accompanying versions of a new fascism), or the experience of citizens could dismiss our hubris as yet another historical collection of neo-Promethean, but essentially ephemeral, follies. Informed choice requires that we examine the specific role of the professions in determining who in this age got what from whom and why.

To see the present clearly, let us imagine the children who will soon play in the ruins of high schools, Hiltons, and hospitals. In these professional castles turned cathedrals, built to protect us against ignorance, discomfort, pain, and death, the children of tomorrow will re-enact in their play the delusions of our Age of Professions, as from ancient castles and cathedrals we reconstruct the crusades of knights against sin and the Turk in the Age of Faith. Children in their games will mingle the Uniquack which now pollutes our language with archaisms inherited from robber barons and cowboys. I see them addressing each other as chairman and secretary rather than as chief and lord. Of course, adults will blush when they slip into managerial pidgin with terms such as policy-making, social planning, and problem-solving.

The Age of Professions will be remembered as the time when politics withered, when voters, guided by professors, entrusted to technocrats the power to legislate needs, the authority to decide who needed what, and a monopoly over the means by which those needs should be met. It will be remembered as the Age of Schooling, when people for one-third of their lives were trained to accumulate needs on prescription and for the other two-thirds were clients of prestigious pushers who managed their habits. It will be remembered as the age when recreational travel meant a packaged gawk at strangers, and intimacy meant training by Masters and Johnson; when formed opinion was a replay of last night's talk-show, and voting an endorsement of a salesman for more of the same.

Future students will be as confused by the supposed differences between capitalist and socialist school, health-care, prison, or transportation systems as today's students are by the claimed differences between justification by works and justification by faith in the late Reformation Christian sects. They will also discover that the professional librarians, surgeons, or supermarket designers in poor or socialist countries toward the end of each decade came to keep the same records, use the same tools, and build the same spaces that their colleagues in rich countries had pioneered at the decade's beginning. Archaeologists will periodize our life-span not by potsherds but by professional fashions, reflected in the mod-trends of United Nations publications.

It would be pretentious to predict whether this age, when needs were shaped by professional design, will be remembered with a smile or a curse. I hope, of course, that it will be remembered as the night when father went on a binge, dissipated the family fortune, and obligated his children to start anew. Sad to say, it will much more probably be remembered as the time when a whole generation's frenzied pursuit of impoverishing wealth rendered all freedoms alienable and, after first turning politics into the organized gripes of welfare recipients, extinguished it in expert totalitarianism.

Professional Dominance

Let us first face the fact that the bodies of specialists that now dominate the creation, adjudication, and satisfaction of needs are a new kind of cartel. And this must be recognized in order to outflank their developing defenses. For we already see the new biocrat hiding behind the benevolent mask of the physician of old; the pedocrat's behavioral aggression is shrugged off as the overzealous, perhaps silly care of the concerned teacher; the personnel manager equipped with a psychological arsenal presents himself in the guise of an old-time foreman. The new specialists, who are usually servicers of those human needs that their specialties have defined, tend to wear the mask of love and to provide some form of care. They are more deeply entrenched than a Byzantine bureaucracy, more international than a world church, more stable than any labor union, endowed with wider competencies than any shaman, and equipped with a tighter hold over those they claim than any mafia.

The new organized specialists must, first, be carefully distinguished from racketeers. Educators, for instance, now tell society what must be learned and write off what has been learned outside school. By this kind of monopoly, which enables tyrannical professions to prevent you from shopping elsewhere and from making your own booze, they at first seem to fit the dictionary definition of gangsters. But gangsters, for their own profit, corner a basic necessity by controlling supplies. Educators and doctors and social workers today—as did priests and lawyers formerly—gain legal power to create the need that, by law, they alone will be allowed to serve. They turn the modern state into a holding corporation of enterprises that facilitate the operation of their self-certified competencies.

Legalized control over work has taken many different forms: soldiers of fortune refused to fight until they got the license to plunder; Lysistrata organized female chattels to enforce peace by refusing sex; doctors in Cos conspired by oath to pass trade secrets only to their offspring; guilds set the curricula, prayers, tests, pilgrimages, and hazings through which Hans Sachs had to pass before he was permitted to shoe his fellow burghers. In capitalist countries, unions attempt to control who shall work what hours for what pay. All these trade associations are attempts by specialists to determine how their kind of work shall be done and by whom. But none of these specialists are professionals in the sense that doctors, for instance, are today. Today's domineering professionals, of whom physicians provide the most striking and painful example, go further: they decide what shall be made, for whom, and how it shall be administered. They claim special, incommunicable knowledge, not just about the way things are and are to be made, but also about the reasons their services ought to be needed. Merchants sell you the goods they stock. Guildsmen guarantee quality. Some craftspeople tailor their product to your measure or fancy. Professionals, however, tell you what you need. They claim the power to prescribe. They not only advertise what is good, but ordain what is right. Neither income, long training, delicate tasks, nor social standing is the mark of the professional. Their income can be low or taxed away, their training compressed into weeks instead of years; their status can approach that of the oldest profession. Rather, what counts is the professional's authority to define a person as a client, to determine that person's need, and to hand that person a prescription which defines this new social role. Unlike the hookers of old, the modern professional is not one who sells what others give for free, but rather one who decides what ought to be sold and must not be given for free.

There is a further distinction between professional power and that of other occupations: professional power springs from a different source. A guild, a union, or a gang forces respect for its interest and rights by a strike, blackmail, or overt violence. In contrast, a profession, like a priesthood, holds power by concession from an elite whose interests it props up. As a priesthood offers the way to salvation in the train of an anointed king, so a profession interprets, protects, and supplies a special this-worldly interest to the constituency of modern rulers. Professional power is a specialized form of the privilege to prescribe what is right for others and what they therefore need. It is the source of prestige and control within the industrial state. This kind of professional power could, of course, come into existence only in societies where elite membership itself is legitimated, if not acquired, by professional status: a society where governing elites are attributed a unique kind of objectivity in defining the moral status of a lack. It fits like a glove the age in which even access to parliament, the house of commons, is in fact limited to those who have acquired the title of master by accumulating knowledge stock in some college. Professional autonomy and license in defining the needs of society are the logical forms that oligarchy takes in a political culture that has replaced the means test by knowledge-stock certificates issued by schools. The professions' power over the work their members do is thus distinct in both scope and origin.

Toward Professional Tyranny

Professional power has also, recently, so changed in degree that two animals of entirely different color now go by the same name. For instance, the practicing and experimenting health scientist consistently evades critical analysis by dressing up in the clothes of yesterday's family doctor. The wandering physician became the medical doctor when he left commerce in drugs to the pharmacist and kept for himself the power to prescribe them. At that moment, he acquired a new kind of authority by uniting three roles in one person: the sapiential authority to advise, instruct, and direct; the moral authority that makes its acceptance not just useful but obligatory; and the charismatic authority that allows the physician to appeal to some supreme interest of his clients that outranks not only conscience but sometimes even the *raison d'état*. This kind of doctor, of course, still exists, but within a modern medical system he is a figure out of the past. A new kind of health scientist is now much more common. He increasingly deals more with cases than with persons; he deals with the breakdown that he can perceive in the case rather than with the complaint of the individual; he protects society's interest rather than the person's. The authorities that, during the liberal age, had coalesced in the individual practitioner in his treatment of a patient are now claimed by the professional corporation in the service of the state. This entity now carves out for itself a social mission.

Only during the last twenty-five years has medicine turned from a liberal into a dominant profession, by obtaining the power to indicate what constitutes a health need for people in general. Health specialists as a corporation have acquired the authority to determine what health care must be provided to society at large. It is no longer the individual professional who imputes a need to the individual client, but a corporate agency that imputes a need to entire classes of people and then claims the mandate to test the complete population in order to identify all who belong to the group of potential patients. And what happens in health care is thoroughly consistent with what goes on in other domains. New pundits constantly jump on the bandwagon of the therapeutic-care provider: educators, social workers, the military, town planners, judges, policemen, and their ilk have obviously made it. They enjoy wide autonomy in creating the diagnostic tools by which they then catch their clients for treatment. Dozens of other need-creators try: international bankers "diagnose" the ills of an African country and then induce it to swallow the prescribed treatment, even though the "patient" might die; security specialists evaluate the loyalty risk in a citizen and then extinguish his private sphere; dog-catchers sell themselves to the public as pest-controllers and claim a monopoly over the lives of stray dogs. The only way to prevent the escalation of needs is a fundamental, political exposure of those illusions that legitimate dominating professions.

Many professions are so well established that they not only exercise tutelage over the citizen-become-client, but also determine the shape of his world-become-ward. The language in which he perceives himself, his perception of rights and freedoms, and his awareness of needs, all derive from professional hegemony.

The difference between craftsman, liberal professional, and the new technocrat can be clarified by comparing their typical reactions to people who neglect their respective advice. If you did not take the craftsman's advice, you were a fool. If you did not take liberal counsel, society blamed you. Now, the profession or the government may be blamed when you escape from the care that your lawyer, teacher, surgeon, or shrink has decided upon for you. Under the pretense of meeting needs on a better and more equitable basis, the service professional has mutated into a crusading philanthropist. The nutritionist prescribes the "right" formula for the infant and the psychiatrist the "right" antidepressant, and the schoolmaster—now acting with the fuller power of "educator"—feels entitled to push his method between you and anything you want to learn. Each new specialty in service production thrives only when the public has accepted and the law has endorsed a new perception of what ought not to exist. Schools expanded in a moralizing crusade against illiteracy, once illiteracy had been defined as an evil. Maternity wards mushroomed to do away with home births.

Professionals claim a monopoly over the definition of deviance and the remedies needed. For example, lawyers assert that they alone have the competence and the legal right to provide assistance in divorce. If you devise a kit for do-it-yourself divorce, you find yourself in a double bind: if you are not a lawyer, you are liable for practicing without a license; if you are a member of the bar, you can be expelled for unprofessional behavior. Professionals also claim secret knowledge about human nature and its weaknesses, knowledge they are also mandated to apply. Gravediggers, for example, did not become members of a profession by calling themselves morticians, by obtaining college credentials, by raising their incomes, or by getting rid of the odor attached to their trade by electing one of themselves president of the Lion's Club. Morticians formed a profession, a dominant and disabling one, when they acquired the muscle to have the police stop your burial if you are not embalmed and boxed by them. In any area where a human need can be imagined, these new disabling professions claim that they are the exclusive wardens of the public good.

Professions as a New Clergy

The transformation of a liberal profession into a dominant one is equivalent to the legal establishment of a church. Physicians transmogrified into biocrats, teachers into gnosocrats, morticians into thanatocrats, are much closer to state-supported clergies than to trade associations. The professional, as teacher of the current brand of scientific orthodoxy, acts as theologian. As moral entrepreneur, he acts the role of priest: he creates the need for his mediation. As crusading helper, he acts the part of the missionary and hunts down the underprivileged. As inquisitor, he outlaws the unorthodox—he imposes his solutions on the recalcitrant who refuse to recognize that they are a problem. This multifaceted investiture, with the task of relieving a specific inconvenience of man's estate, turns each profession into the analogue of an established cult. The public acceptance of domineering professions is thus essentially a political event. The new profession creates a new hierarchy, new clients and outcasts, and a new strain on the budget. But each new establishment of professional legitimacy also means that the political tasks of lawmaking, judicial review, and executive power lose more of their proper character and independence. Public affairs pass from the layperson's elected peers into the hands of a self-accrediting elite.

When medicine recently outgrew its liberal restraints, it invaded legislation by establishing public norms. Physicians had always determined what constituted disease; dominant medicine now determines what diseases society shall not tolerate. Medicine has invaded the courts. Physicians had always diagnosed who was sick; dominant medicine, however, brands those who must be treated. Liberal practitioners prescribed a cure; dominant medicine has public powers of correction: it decides what shall be done with or to the sick. In a democracy, the power to make laws, execute them, and achieve public justice must derive from the citizens themselves. This citizen control over the key powers has been restricted, weakened, and sometimes abolished by the rise of church-like professions. Government by a congress that bases its decisions on expert opinions of such professions might be government for, but never by, the people. This is not the place to investigate the intent with which political rule was thus weakened; it is sufficient to indicate the professional disqualification of lay opinion as a necessary condition for this subversion.

Citizen liberties are grounded in the rule that excludes hearsay from testimony on which public decisions are based. What people can see for themselves and interpret is the common ground for binding rules. Opinions, beliefs, inferences, or persuasions ought not to stand when in conflict with the eyewitness—ever. Expert elites could become dominant professions only by a piecemeal erosion and final reversal of this rule. In the legislature and courts, the rule against hearsay evidence is now, *de facto*, suspended, in favor of the opinions proffered by the members of these self-accredited elites.

But let us not confuse the public use of expert factual knowledge with a profession's corporate exercise of normative judgment. When a craftsman, such as a gunmaker, was called into court as an expert to reveal to the jury the secrets of his trade, he apprenticed the jury to his craft on the spot. He demonstrated visibly from which barrel the bullet had come. Today, most experts play a different role. The dominant professional provides jury or legislature with his fellow initiate's opinion rather than with factual evidence and a skill. He calls for a suspension of the hearsay rule and inevitably undermines the rule of law. Thus, democratic power is ineluctably abridged.

The Hegemony of Imputed Needs

Professions could not have become dominant and disabling unless people had been ready to experience as a lack that which the expert imputed to them as a need. Their mutual dependence as tutor and charge has become resistant to analysis because it has been obscured by corrupted language. Good old words have been made into branding irons that claim wardship for experts over home, shop, store, and the space or ether between them. Language, the most fundamental of commons, is thus polluted by twisted strands of jargon, each under the control of another profession. The disseizin of words, the depletion of ordinary language and its degradation into bureaucratic terminology, parallel in a more intimately debasing manner that particular form of environmental degradation that dispossesses people of their usefulness unless they are gainfully employed. Possible changes in design, attitudes, and laws that would retrench professional dominance cannot be proposed unless we become more sensitive to the misnomers behind which this dominance hides.

When I learned to speak, "problems" existed only in math or chess; "solutions" were saline or legal, and "need" was mainly used as a verb. The expressions "I have a problem" or "I have a need" both sounded silly. As I grew into my teens and Hitler worked at "solutions," the "social problem" also spread. "Problem" children of ever newer shades were discovered among the poor, as social workers learned to brand their prey and to standardize their "needs." Need, used as a noun, became the fodder on which professions fattened into dominance. Poverty was modernized. Management translated poverty from an experience into a measure. The poor became the "needy."

During the second half of my life, to be "needy" became respectable. Computable and imputable needs moved up the social ladder. It ceased to be a sign of poverty to have needs. Income opened new registers of need. Spock, Comfort, and the vulgarizers of Nader trained laymen to shop for solutions to problems they learned to cook up according to professional recipes. Education qualified graduates to climb to ever more rarefied heights, and to implant and cultivate there ever newer strains of hybridized needs. Prescriptions increased and competences shrank. In medicine, for example, ever more pharmacologically active drugs went on prescription, and people lost their will and ability to cope with indisposition or even discomfort. In American supermarkets, where it is estimated that about 1,500 new products appear each year, less than twenty percent survive more than one year on the shelves, the remainder having proved unsellable, faddish, risky, or unprofitable, or obsolete in competition with new models. Therefore, consumers are increasingly forced to seek guidance from professional consumer protectors.

Furthermore, the rapid turnover of products renders wants shallow and plastic. Paradoxically, then, high-aggregate consumption resulting from engineered needs fosters growing consumer indifference to specific, potentially felt wants. Increasingly, needs are created by the advertising slogan and by purchases made by order from the registrar, beautician, gynecologist, and dozens of other prescribing diagnosticians. The need to be formally taught how to need, be this by advertising, prescription, or guided discussion in the collective or in the commune, appears in any culture where decisions and actions are no longer the result of personal experience in satisfaction, and the adaptive consumer cannot but substitute learned for felt needs. As people become apt pupils in learning how to need, the ability to shape wants from experienced satisfaction becomes a rare competence of the very rich or the seriously undersupplied. As needs are broken down into ever smaller component parts, each managed by an appropriate specialist, the consumer experiences difficulty in integrating the separate offerings of his various tutors into a meaningful whole that could be desired with commitment and possessed with pleasure. The income managers, life-style counselors, consciousness-raisers, academic advisers, food-fad experts, sensitivity developers, and others like them clearly perceive the new possibilities for management and move in to match packaged commodities to the splintered needs.

Used as a noun, "need" is the individual offprint of a professional pattern; it is a plastic-foam replica of the mold in which professionals cast their staple; it is the advertised shape of the brood cells out of which consumers are produced. To be ignorant or unconvinced of one's own needs has become the unforgivable antisocial act. The good citizen is one who imputes standardized needs to himself with such conviction that he drowns out any desire for alternatives, much less for the renunciation of needs.

When I was born, before Stalin and Hitler and Roosevelt came to power, only the rich, hypochondriacs, and members of elite unions spoke of their need for medical care when their temperatures rose. Doctors then, in response, could not do much more than grandmothers had done. In medicine, the first mutation of needs came with sulfa drugs and antibiotics. As the control of infections became a simple and effective routine, drugs went more and more on prescription. Assignment of the sick-role became a medical monopoly. The person who felt ill had to go to the clinic to be labeled with a disease-name and to be legitimately declared a member of the minority of the so-called "sick:" people excused from work, entitled to help, put under doctor's orders, and enjoined to heal in order to become useful again. Paradoxically, as pharmacological technique—tests and drugs—became so predictable and cheap that one could have dispensed with the physician, society enacted laws and police regulations to restrict the free use of those procedures that science had simplified, and placed them on the prescription list.

The second mutation of medical needs happened when the sick ceased to be a minority. Today, few people eschew doctors' orders for any length of time. In Italy, the United States, France, or Belgium, one out of every two citizens is being watched simultaneously by several health professionals, who treat, advise, or at least observe him or her. The object of such specialized care is, more often than not, a condition of teeth, womb, emotions, blood pressure, or hormone levels that the patient himself does not feel. Patients are no more in the minority. Now, the minority are those deviants who somehow escape from any and all patient-roles. This minority is made up of the poor, the peasants, the recent immigrants, and sundry others who, sometimes on their own volition, have gone medically AWOL. Just twenty years ago, it was a sign of normal health—which was assumed to be good—to get along without a doctor. The same status of nonpatient is now indicative of poverty or dissidence. Even the status of the hypochondriac has changed. For the doctor in the forties, this was the label applied to the gate-crashers in his office—the designation reserved for the imaginary sick. Now, doctors refer to the minority who flee them by the same name: hypochondriacs are the imaginary healthy. To be plugged into a professional system as a lifelong client is no longer a stigma that sets apart the disabled person from citizens at large. We now live in a society organized for deviant majorities and their keepers. To be an active client of several professionals provides you with a well-defined place within the realm of consumers, for the sake of whom our society functions. Thus, the transformation of medicine from a liberal consulting profession into a dominant, disabling profession has immeasurably increased the number of the needy.

At this critical moment, imputed needs move into a third mutation. They coalesce into what the experts call a "multidisciplinary problem," necessitating, therefore, a multi-professional solution. First, the proliferation of commodities, each tending to turn into a requirement, has effectively trained the consumer to need on command. Next, the progressive fragmentation of needs into ever smaller and unconnected parts has made the client dependent on professional judgment for the blending of his needs into a meaningful whole. The auto industry provides a good example. By the end of the sixties, the advertised optional equipment needed to make a basic Ford desirable had been multiplied immensely. But, contrary to the customer's expectations, this "optional" flim-flam is in fact installed on the assembly line of the Detroit factory, and the shopper in Plains is left with a choice between a few packaged samples that are shipped at random: he can either buy the convertible that he wants but with the green seats he hates, or he can humor his girlfriend with leopard-skin seats at the cost of buying an unwanted paisley hardtop.

Finally, the client is trained to need a team approach to receive what his guardians consider "satisfactory treatment." Personal services that improve the consumer illustrate the point. Therapeutic affluence has exhausted the available lifetime of many whom service professionals diagnose as standing in need of more. The intensity of the service economy has made the time needed for the consumption of pedagogical, medical, and social treatments increasingly scarce. Time scarcity may soon turn into the major obstacle to the consumption of prescribed, and often publicly financed, services. Signs of such scarcity become evident from one's early years. Already in kindergarten, the child is subjected to management by a team made up of such specialists as the allergist, speech pathologist, pediatrician, child psychologist, social worker, physical-education instructor, and teacher. By forming such a pedocratic team, many different professionals attempt to share the time that has become the major limiting factor to the imputation of further needs. For the adult, it is not the school but the workplace where the packaging of services focuses. The personnel manager, labor educator, in-service trainer, insurance planner, and consciousness-raiser find it more profitable to share the worker's time than to compete for it. A need-less citizen would be highly suspicious. People are told that they need their jobs not so much for the money as for the services they get. The commons are extinguished and replaced by a new placenta built of funnels that deliver professional services. Life is paralyzed in permanent intensive care.

Enabling Distinctions

The disabling of the citizen through professional dominance is completed through the power of illusion. Hopes of religious salvation are displaced by expectations that center on the state as supreme manager of professional services. Each of many special priesthoods claims competence to define public issues in terms of specific serviceable problems. The acceptance of this claim legitimates the docile recognition of imputed lacks on the part of the layman, whose world turns into an echo-chamber of needs. The satisfaction of self-defined preference is sacrificed to the fulfillment of educated needs. This dominance of engineered and managed needs is reflected in the skyline of the city: professional buildings look down on the crowds that shuttle between them in a continual pilgrimage to the new cathedrals of health, education, and welfare. Healthy homes are transformed into hygienic apartments where one cannot be born, cannot be sick, and cannot die decently. Not only are helpful neighbors a vanishing species, but also liberal doctors who make house calls. Workplaces fit for apprenticeship turn into opaque mazes of corridors that permit access only to functionaries equipped with "identities" in mica holders, pinned to their lapels. A world designed for service deliveries is the utopia of citizens turned into welfare recipients.

The prevailing addiction to imputable needs on the part of the rich, and the paralyzing fascination with needs on the part of the poor, would indeed be irreversible if people actually fitted the calculus of needs. But this is not so. Beyond a certain level of intensity, medicine engenders helplessness and disease; education turns into the major generator of a disabling division of labor; fast transportation systems turn urbanized people for about one-sixth of their waking hours into passengers, and for an equal amount of time into members of the road gang that works to pay Ford, Exxon, and the highway department. The threshold at which medicine, education, and transportation turn into counterproductive tools has been reached in all the countries of the world with per capita incomes comparable at least to those prevalent in Cuba. In all countries examined, and contrary to the illusions propagated by the orthodoxies of both East and West, this specific counterproductivity bears no relation to the kind of school, vehicle, or health organization now used. It sets in when the capital intensity of the production process passes a critical threshold.

Our major institutions have acquired the uncanny power to subvert the very purposes for which they were originally engineered and financed. Under the rule of our most prestigious professions, our institutional tools have as their principal product paradoxical counterproductivity—the systematic disabling of the citizenry. A city built around wheels becomes inappropriate for feet, and no increase in the number of wheels can overcome the engineered immobility of such cripples. Autonomous action is paralyzed by a surfeit of commodities and treatments. But this does not represent simply a net loss of satisfactions that do not happen to fit into the industrial age. The impotence to produce use-values ultimately renders counter-purposive the very commodities meant to replace them. The car, the doctor, the school, and the manager are then commodities that have turned into destructive nuisances for the consumer, and retain net value only for the provider of services.

Why are there no rebellions against the coalescence of late industrial society into one huge disabling service-delivery system? The chief explanation must be sought in the illusion-generating power that these same systems possess. Besides doing technical things to body and mind, professionally attended institutions also function as powerful rituals that generate credence in the things their managers promise. Besides teaching Johnny to read, schools also teach him that learning from teachers is "better," and that without compulsory schools, fewer books would be read by the poor. Besides providing locomotion, the bus, just as much as the sedan, reshapes the environment and puts walking out of step. Besides providing help in avoiding taxes, lawyers also convey the notion that laws solve problems. An ever-growing part of our major institutions' function is the cultivation and maintenance of three sets of illusions which turn the citizen into a client to be saved by experts.

Congestion versus Paralysis

The first enslaving illusion is the idea that people are born to be consumers and that they can attain any of their goals by purchasing goods and services. This illusion is due to an educated blindness to the worth of use-values in the total economy. In none of the economic models serving as national guidelines is there a variable to account for nonmarketable use-values, any more than there is a variable for nature's perennial contribution. Yet, there is no economy that would not collapse immediately if use-value production contracted beyond a point; for example, if homemaking were done only for wages, or intercourse engaged in only at a fee. What people do or make but will not or cannot put up for sale is as immeasurable and as invaluable for the economy as the oxygen they breathe.

The illusion that economic models can ignore use-values springs from the assumption that those activities which we designate by intransitive verbs can be indefinitely replaced by institutionally defined staples referred to as nouns: "education" substituted for "I learn," "health care" for "I heal," "transportation" for "I move," "television" for "I play."

The confusion of personal and standardized values has spread throughout most domains. Under professional leadership, use-values are dissolved, rendered obsolete, and finally deprived of their distinctive nature. Love and institutional care become coterminous. Ten years of running a farm can be thrown into a pedagogical mixer and made equivalent to a high-school degree.

Things picked up at random and hatched in the freedom of the street are added as "educational experience" to things funneled into pupils' heads. The knowledge-accountants seem unaware that the two activities, like oil and water, mix only as long as they are osterized by an educator's perception. Gangs of crusading need-creators could not continue to tax us, nor could they spend our resources on their tests, networks, and other nostrums, if we did not remain paralyzed by this kind of greedy belief.

The usefulness of staples, or packaged commodities, is intrinsically limited by two boundaries that must not be confused. First, queues will sooner or later stop the operation of any system that produces needs faster than the corresponding commodity, and second, dependence on commodities will sooner or later so determine needs that the autonomous production of a functional analogue will be paralyzed. The usefulness of commodities is limited by *congestion* and *paralysis*. Congestion and paralysis are both results of escalation in any sector of production, albeit results of a very different kind. Congestion, which is a measure of the degree to which staples get in their own way, explains why mass transportation by private car in Manhattan would be useless; it does not explain why people work hard to buy and insure cars that cannot move them. Even less does congestion alone explain why people become so dependent on vehicles that they are paralyzed and cannot take to their feet.

People become prisoners to time-consuming acceleration, stupefying education, and sick-making medicine because, beyond a certain threshold of intensity, dependence on a bill of industrial and professional goods destroys human potential and does so in a specific way. Only up to a point can commodities replace what people make or do on their own. Only within limits can exchange-values satisfactorily replace use-values. Beyond this point, further production serves the interests of the professional producer—who has imputed the need to the consumer—and leaves the consumer befuddled and giddy, albeit richer. Needs satisfied rather than merely fed must be determined to a significant degree by the pleasure that is derived from the remembrance of personal autonomous action. There are boundaries beyond which commodities cannot be multiplied without disabling their consumer for this self-affirmation in action.

Packages alone inevitably frustrate the consumer when their delivery paralyzes him or her. The measure of well-being in a society is thus never an equation in which these two modes of production are matched; it is always a balance that results when use-values and commodities fruitfully mesh in synergy. Only up to a point can heteronomous production of a commodity enhance and complement the autonomous production of the corresponding personal purpose. Beyond this point, the synergy between the two modes of production paradoxically turns against the purpose for which both use-value and commodity were intended. Occasionally, this is not clearly seen because the mainstream ecology movement tends to obscure the point. For example, atomic-energy reactors have been widely criticized because their radiation is a threat, or because they foster technocratic controls. So far, however, only very few have dared to criticize them because they add to the energy glut. The paralysis of human action by socially destructive energy quanta has not yet been accepted as an argument for reducing the call for energy. Similarly, the inexorable limits to growth that are built into any service agency are still widely ignored. And yet, it ought to be evident that the institutionalization of health care tends to make people into unhealthy marionettes, and that lifelong education fosters a culture of programmed people. Ecology will provide guidelines for a feasible form of modernity only when it is recognized that a man-made environment designed for commodities reduces personal aliveness to the point where the commodities themselves lose their value as means for personal satisfaction. Without this insight, industrial technology that was cleaner and less aggressive would be used for now-impossible levels of frustrating enrichment.

It would be a mistake to attribute counterproductivity essentially to the negative externalities of economic growth, to exhaustion, pollution, and various forms of congestion. This leads us to confuse the congestion by which things get in their own way with the paralysis of the person who can no longer exercise his or her autonomy in an environment designed for things. The fundamental reason that market intensity leads to counterproductivity must be sought in the relationship between the monopoly of commodities and human needs. This monopoly extends further than what usually goes by the name. A commercial monopoly merely corners the market for one brand of whiskey or car. An industry-wide cartel can restrict freedom further: it can corner all mass transportation in favor of internal combustion engines, as General Motors did when it purchased the Los Angeles trolleys. You can escape the first by sticking to rum and the second by purchasing a bicycle. I use the term "radical monopoly" to designate something else: the substitution of an industrial product or a professional service for a useful activity in which people engage or would like to engage. A radical monopoly paralyzes autonomous action in favor of professional deliveries. The more completely vehicles dislocate people, the more traffic managers will be needed and the more powerless people will be to walk home. This radical monopoly would accompany high-speed traffic even if motors were powered by sunshine and vehicles were spun of air. The longer each person is in the grip of education, the less time and inclination he has for browsing and exploration. At some point in every domain, the amount of goods delivered so degrades the environment for personal action that the possible synergy between use-values and commodities turns negative. Paradoxical, or specific, counterproductivity sets in. I will use this term whenever the impotence resulting from the substitution of a commodity for a value in use turns this very commodity into a disvalue in the pursuit of the satisfaction it was meant to provide.

Industrial versus Convivial Tools

Man ceases to be recognizable as one of his kind when he can no longer shape his own needs by the more or less competent use of those tools his culture provides. Throughout history, most tools were labor-intensive means that could be employed to satisfy the user of the tool, and were used in domestic production. Only marginally were shovels or hammers used to produce pyramids or a surplus for gift-exchange, and even more rarely to produce things for the market. Occasions for the extraction of profits were limited. Most work was done to create use-values not destined for exchange. But technological progress has been consistently applied to develop a very different kind of tool: it has pressed the tool primarily into the production of marketable staples. At first, during the industrial revolution, the new technology reduced the worker on the job to a Charlie Chaplin in *Modern Times*. At this early stage, however, the industrial mode of production did not yet paralyze people when they were off the job. Now, women or men who have come to depend almost entirely on deliveries of standardized fragments produced by tools operated by anonymous others have ceased to find the same direct satisfaction in the use of tools that stimulated the evolution of man and his cultures. Although their needs and their consumption have multiplied many times, their satisfaction in handling tools has become rare, and they have ceased to live a life for which their organism acquired its form. At best, they barely survive, even though they do so surrounded by glitter. Their life-span has become a chain of needs that have been met for the sake of an ulterior striving for satisfaction. Ultimately, man-the-passive-consumer loses even the ability to discriminate between living and survival. The gamble on insurance and the gleeful expectation of rations and therapies take the place of enjoyment. In such company, it becomes easy to forget that satisfaction and joy can result only as long as personal aliveness and engineered provisions are kept in balance while a goal is pursued.

The delusion that tools in the service of market-oriented institutions can with impunity destroy the conditions for convivial and personally manageable means permits the extinction of "aliveness" by conceiving of technological progress as a kind of engineering product that licenses more professional domination. This delusion says that tools, in order to become more efficient in the pursuit of a specific purpose, inevitably become more complex and inscrutable: one thinks of cockpits and cranes. Therefore, it would seem that modern tools would require special operators who were highly trained and who alone could be securely trusted. Actually, just the opposite is usually true, and necessarily so. As techniques multiply and become more specific, their use often requires less complex judgments.

They no longer require that trust on the part of the client on which the autonomy of the liberal professional and even that of the craftsman was built. However far medicine has advanced, only a tiny fraction of the total volume of demonstrably useful medical services necessitates advanced training in an intelligent person. From a social point of view, we ought to reserve the designation "technical progress" for instances in which new tools expand the capacity and the effectiveness of a wider range of people, especially when new tools permit the more autonomous production of use-values.

There is nothing inevitable about the expanding professional monopoly over new technology. The great inventions of the last hundred years, such as new metals, ball-bearings, some building materials, electronics, and some tests and remedies, are capable of increasing the power of both the heteronomous and the autonomous modes of production. In fact, however, most new technology has not been incorporated into convivial equipment but into institutional packages and complexes. The professionals rather consistently have used industrial production to establish a radical monopoly by means of technology's obvious power to serve its manager. Counterproductivity due to the paralysis of use-value production is fostered by this notion of technological progress.

There is no simple "technological imperative" which requires that ball-bearings be used in motorized vehicles or that electronics be used to control the brain. The institutions of high-speed traffic and of mental health are not the necessary result of ball-bearings or electronics. Their functions are determined by the needs they are supposed to serve—needs that are overwhelmingly imputed and reinforced by disabling professions. This is a point that the young Turks in the professions seem to overlook when they justify their institutional allegiance by presenting themselves as the publicly appointed ministers of a technological progress that must be domesticated.

The same subservience to the idea of progress conceives of engineering principally as a contribution to institutional effectiveness. Scientific research is highly financed, but only if it can be applied for military use or for further professional domination. Alloys which make bicycles both stronger and lighter are a fall-out of research designed to make jets faster and weapons deadlier. But the results of most research go solely into industrial tools, thus making already huge machines even more complex and inscrutable. Because of this bias on the part of scientists and engineers, a major trend is strengthened: needs for autonomous action are precluded, while those for the acquisition of commodities are multiplied. Convivial tools which facilitate the individual's enjoyment of use-values—without or with only minimal supervision by policemen, physicians, or inspectors—are polarized at two extremes: poor Asian workers and rich students and professors are the two kinds of people who ride bicycles. Perhaps without being conscious of their good fortune, both enjoy being free from this second illusion.

Recently, some groups of professionals, government agencies, and international organizations have begun to explore, develop, and advocate small-scale, intermediate technology. These efforts might be interpreted as an attempt to avoid the more obvious vulgarities of a technological imperative. But most of the new technology designed for self-help in health care, education, or home building is only an alternative model of high-intensity dependence commodities. For example, experts are asked to design new medicine cabinets that allow people to follow the doctor's orders over the telephone. Women are taught to examine their breasts to provide work for the surgeon. Cubans are given paid leave from work to erect their prefabricated houses. The enticing prestige of professional products, as they become cheaper, ends by making rich and poor more alike. Both Bolivians and Swedes feel equally backward, underprivileged, and exploited, to the degree that they learn without the supervision of certified teachers, keep healthy without the check-ups of a physician, and move about without a motorized crutch.

Liberties versus Rights

The third disabling illusion looks to experts for limits to growth. Entire populations socialized to need on command are assumed to be ready to be told what they do not need. The same multinational agents that for a generation imposed an international standard of bookkeeping, deodorants, and energy consumption on rich and poor alike now sponsor the Club of Rome. Obediently, UNESCO gets into the act and trains experts in the regionalization of imputed needs. For their own imputed good, the rich are thereby programmed to pay for more costly professional dominance at home, and to provide the poor with assigned needs of a cheaper and tighter brand. The brightest of the new professionals see clearly that growing scarcity pushes controls over needs ever upward. The central planning of output-optimal decentralization has become the most prestigious job of 1978. But what is not yet recognized is that this new illusory salvation by professionally decreed limits confuses liberties and rights.

In each of the seven United-Nations-defined world regions, a new clergy is being trained to preach the appropriate style of austerity drafted by the new need-designers. Consciousness-raisers roam through local communities, inciting people to meet the decentralized production goals that have been assigned to them. Milking the family goat was a liberty until more ruthless planning made it a duty to contribute the yield to the GNP.

The synergy of autonomous and heteronomous production is reflected in society's balance of liberties and rights. Liberties protect use-values as rights protect the access to commodities. And just as commodities can extinguish the possibility of producing use-values and turn into impoverishing wealth, so the professional definition of rights can extinguish liberties and establish a tyranny that smothers people underneath their rights.

The confusion is revealed with special clarity when one considers the experts on health. Health encompasses two aspects: liberties and rights. It designates the area of autonomy within which a person exercises control over his own biological states and over the conditions of his immediate environment. Simply stated, health is identical with the degree of lived freedom. Therefore, those concerned with the public good should work to guarantee the equitable distribution of health as freedom which, in turn, depends on environmental conditions that only organized political efforts can achieve. Beyond a certain level of intensity, professional health care, however equitably distributed, will smother health-as-freedom. In this fundamental sense, the care of health is a matter of well-protected liberty.

As is evident, such a notion of health implies a principled commitment to inalienable freedoms. To understand this, one must distinguish clearly between civil liberty and civil rights. The liberty to act without restraint from government has a wider scope than the civil rights the state may enact to guarantee that people will have equal powers to obtain certain goods and services.

Civil liberties ordinarily do not force others to act in accord with one's own wishes. I have the freedom to speak and publish my opinion, but no specific newspaper is obliged to print it, nor are fellow citizens required to read it. I am free to paint as I see beauty, but no museum has to buy my canvas. At the same time, however, the state as guarantor of liberty can and does enact laws that protect the equal rights without which its members would not enjoy their freedoms. Such rights give meaning and reality to equality, while liberties give possibility and shape to freedom. One certain way to extinguish the freedoms to speak, to learn, to heal, or to care is to delimit them by transmogrifying civil rights into civic duties. The precise character of this third illusion is to believe that the publicly sponsored pursuit of rights leads inevitably to the protection of liberties. In reality, as society gives professionals the legitimacy to define rights, citizen freedoms evaporate.

Equity in Useful Unemployment

At present, every new need that is professionally certified translates sooner or later into a right. The political pressure for the enactment of each right generates new jobs and commodities. Each new commodity degrades an activity by which people so far have been able to cope on their own; each new job takes away legitimacy from work so far done by the unemployed. The power of professions to measure what shall be good, right, and done warps the desire, willingness, and ability of the "common" man to live within his means.

As soon as all law students currently registered at United States law schools are graduated, the number of United States lawyers will increase by about fifty percent. Judicare will complement Medicare, as legal insurance increasingly turns into the kind of necessity that medical insurance is now. When the right of the citizen to a lawyer has been established, settling the dispute in the pub will be branded unenlightened or antisocial, as home births are now. Already, the right of each citizen of Detroit to live in a home that has been professionally wired turns the auto-electrician who installs his own plugs into a lawbreaker. The loss of one liberty after another to be useful when out of a job or outside professional control is the unnamed but also the most resented experience that comes with modernized poverty. By now, the most significant privilege of high social status might well be some vestige of freedom for useful unemployment that is increasingly denied to the great majority. The insistence on the right to be taken care of and supplied has almost turned into the right of industries and professions to conquer clients, to supply them with their product, and by their deliveries to obliterate the environmental conditions that make unemployed activities useful. Thus, for the time being, the struggle for an equitable distribution of the time and the power to be useful to oneself and to others, outside employment or the draft, has been effectively paralyzed. Work done off the paid job is looked down upon, if not ignored. Autonomous activity threatens the employment level, generates deviance, and detracts from the GNP: therefore, it is only improperly called "work." Labor no longer means effort or toil, but the mysterious mate wedded to productive investments in-plant. Work no longer means the creation of a value perceived by the worker, but mainly a job, which is a social relationship. Unemployment means sad idleness, rather than the freedom to do things that are useful for oneself or for one's neighbor. An active woman who runs a house and brings up children and takes in those of others is distinguished from a woman who *works*, no matter how useless or damaging the product of this work might be. Activity, effort, achievement, or service outside a hierarchical relationship and unmeasured by professional standards threatens a commodity-intensive society. The generation of use-values that escape effective measurement limits not only the need for more commodities, but also the jobs that create them and the paychecks needed to buy them.

What counts in a market-intensive society is not the effort to please or the pleasure that flows from that effort, but the coupling of the labor force with capital. What counts is not the achievement of satisfaction that flows from action, but the status of the social relationship that commands production—that is, the job, situation, post, or appointment. In the Middle Ages, there was no salvation outside the Church, and theologians had a hard time explaining what God did with those pagans who were visibly virtuous or saintly. Similarly, in contemporary society effort is not productive unless it is done at the behest of a boss, and economists have a hard time dealing with the obvious usefulness of people when they are outside the corporate control of a corporation, volunteer agency, or labor camp. Work is productive, respectable, worthy of the citizen only when the work process is planned, monitored, and controlled by a professional agent, who ensures that the work meets a certified need in a standardized fashion. In an advanced industrial society, it becomes almost impossible to seek, or even to imagine, unemployment as a condition for autonomous, useful work. The infrastructure of society is so arranged that only the job gives access to the tools of production, and this monopoly of commodity production over the generation of use-values turns even more stringent as the state takes over. Only with a license may you teach a child; only at a clinic may you set a broken bone. Housework, handicrafts, subsistence agriculture, radical technology, learning exchanges, and the like are degraded into activities for the idle, the unproductive, the very poor, or the very rich. A society that fosters intense dependence on commodities thus turns its unemployed into either its poor or its dependents. In 1945, for each American social-security recipient there were still thirty-five workers on the job. In 1977, 3.2 employed workers have to support one such retiree, who is himself dependent on many more services than his retired grandfather could have imagined.

Henceforth, the quality of a society and of its culture will depend on the status of its unemployed: will they be the most representative productive citizens, or will they be dependents? The choice or crisis again seems clear. On the one hand, advanced industrial society can degenerate into a holding operation harking back to the dream of the sixties: into a well-rationed distribution system that doles out decreasing commodities and jobs and trains its citizens for more standardized consumption and more powerless work. This is the attitude reflected in the policy proposals of most governments at present, from Germany to China, albeit with a fundamental difference in degree: the richer the country, the more urgent it seems to ration access to jobs and to impede useful unemployment that would threaten the volume of the labor market. The inverse, of course, is equally possible: a modern society in which frustrated workers organize to protect the freedom of people to be useful outside the activities that result in the production of commodities. But again, this social alternative depends on a new, rational, and cynical competence of the common man when faced with the professional imputation of needs.

Outflanking the New Professional

Today, professional power is clearly threatened by increasing evidence of the counterproductivity of its output. People are beginning to see that such hegemony deprives them of their right to politics. The symbolic power of experts, which, while defining needs, eviscerates personal competence, is now seen to be more perilous than their technical capability, which is confined to servicing the needs they create. Simultaneously, one hears the repeated call for the enactment of legislation that might lead us beyond an age dominated by the professional ethos: the demand that professional and bureaucratic licensing be replaced by the investiture of elected citizens, rather than altered by the inclusion of consumer representatives on licensing boards; the demand that prescription rules in pharmacies, school curricula, and other pretentious supermarkets be relaxed; the demand for the protection of *productive* liberties; the demand for the right to practice without a license; the demand for public utilities that facilitate client evaluation of all practitioners who work for money. In response to these threats, the major professional establishments, each in its own way, use three fundamental strategies to shore up the erosion of their legitimacy and power.

The Self-Critical Hooker

The first approach is represented by the Club of Rome. Fiat, Volkswagen, and Ford pay economists, ecologists, and experts in social control to identify the products industries ought not to produce, in order to strengthen the industrial system. Also, doctors in the Club of Kos now recommend that surgery, radiation, and chemotherapy be abandoned in the treatment of most cancers, since these treatments usually prolong and intensify suffering without adding to the life-span of the treated. Lawyers and dentists promise to police as never before the competence, decency, and rates of their fellow professionals.

A variant of this approach is seen in some individuals, or their organizations, who challenge the American Bar Association, American Medical Association, and other power brokers of the establishment. These claim to be radical because (1) they advise consumers against the interests of the majority of their peers; (2) they tutor laymen on how to behave on hospital, university, or police governing boards; and (3) they occasionally testify to legislative committees on the uselessness of procedures proposed by the professions and demanded by the public. For example, in a province of Western Canada, doctors prepared a report on some two dozen medical procedures for which the legislature was considering a budget increase. All the procedures were costly, and the doctors pointed out that they were also very painful, that many were dangerous, and that none could be proved effective. For the time being, the legislators refused to act on such medical advice, a failure that, provisionally, tends to reinforce the belief in the necessity of *professional* protection against professional hubris.

Professional self-policing is useful principally in catching the grossly incompetent—the butcher or the outright charlatan. But, as has been shown again and again, it only protects the inept and cements the dependence of the public on their services. The "critical" doctor, the "radical" lawyer, or the "advocacy" architect seduces clients away from his colleagues, who are less aware than he of the vagaries of fashion. First, liberal professions sold the public on the need for their services by promising to watch over the poorer laymen's schooling, ethics, or in-service training. Then dominant professions insisted on their rightful duty to guide and further disable the public by organizing into clubs that brandish the high consciousness of ecological, economic, and social constraints. Such action inhibits the further extension of the professional sector but strengthens public dependence within that sector. The idea that professionals have a *right* to serve the public is thus of very recent origin. Their struggle to establish and legitimate this corporate right becomes one of our most oppressive social threats.

The Alliance of Hawkers

The second strategy seeks to organize and coordinate professional response in a manner that is purportedly more faithful to the multifaceted character of human problems. Also, this approach seeks to utilize ideas borrowed from systems analysis and operations research in order to provide more national and all-encompassing solutions. An example of what this means in practice can be taken from Canada. Four years ago, the Canadian minister of health launched a campaign to convince the public that spending more money on physicians would not change the country's patterns of disease and death. He pointed out that premature loss of life was due overwhelmingly to three factors: accidents, mostly in motor vehicles; heart disease and lung cancer, which doctors are notoriously powerless to heal; and suicide combined with murder, phenomena that are outside medical control. The minister called for new approaches to health and for the retrenchment of medicine. The task of protecting, restoring, or consoling those made sick by the destructive life-style and environment typical of contemporary Canada was taken up by a great variety of new and old professions. Architects discovered that they had a mission to improve Canadians' health; dog control was found to be an interdepartmental problem calling for new specialists. A new corporate biocracy intensified control over the organisms of Canadians with a thoroughness that the old iatrocracy could hardly have imagined. The slogan "Better spend money in order to stay healthy than on doctors when you get sick" can now be recognized as the hawking of new hookers who want the money spent on them.

The practice of medicine in the United States illustrates a similar dynamic. There, a coordinated approach to the health of Americans has become enormously expensive without being especially effective. In 1950, the typical wage-earner transferred less than two weeks' pay per year to professional health care. In 1976, the proportion was up to around five to seven weeks' pay per year: buying a new Ford, one now pays more for worker hygiene than for the metal the car contains. Yet, with all this effort and expense, the life expectancy of the *adult* male population has not sensibly changed in the last one hundred years. It is lower than in many poor countries and has been declining slowly but steadily for the last twenty years.

Where disease patterns have changed for the better, it has been due principally to the adoption of a healthier life-style, especially in diet. To a small degree, inoculations and the routine administration of such simple interventions as antibiotics, contraceptives, or Carman tubes have contributed to the decline of certain diseases. But such procedures do not postulate the need for professional services. People cannot become healthier by being more firmly wedded to a medical profession, yet many "radical" doctors call for just such an increased biocracy. They seem to be unaware that a more rational "problem-solving" approach is simply another version—though perhaps a more sophisticated one—of affirmative action.

The Professionalization of the Client

The third strategy to make dominant professions survive is this year's radical chic. As the prophets of the sixties drooled about development on the doorsteps of affluence, these myth-makers mouth about the self-help of professionalized clients.

In the United States alone, about 2,700 books have appeared since 1965 that teach you how to be your own patient, so that you need see the doctor only when it is worthwhile for him. Some books recommend that only after due training and examination should graduates in self-medication be empowered to buy aspirin and dispense it to their children. Others suggest that professionalized patients should receive preferential rates in hospitals and that they should benefit from lower insurance premiums. Only women with a license to practice home birth should have their children outside hospitals, since such professional mothers can, if necessary, be sued for malpractice. I have seen a "radical" proposal that such a license to birth be obtained under feminist rather than medical auspices. The professional dream of rooting each hierarchy of needs in the grassroots goes under the banner of self-help. At present, it is promoted by the new tribe of experts in self-help who have replaced the experts in development of the sixties. The universal professionalization of clients is their aim. American building experts who last fall invaded Mexico serve as an example of the new crusade. About two years ago, a Boston professor of architecture came to Mexico for a vacation. A Mexican friend of mine took him beyond the airport, where, during the last twelve years, a new city had grown up. From a few huts, it had mushroomed into a community three times the size of Cambridge, Massachusetts. My friend, also an architect, wanted to show him the thousands of examples of peasant ingenuity, with patterns, structures, and uses of refuse not in and therefore not derivable from textbooks. He should not have been surprised that his colleague took several hundred rolls of pictures of these brilliant amateur inventions that make the two-million-person slum work. The pictures were analyzed in Cambridge, and by the end of the year, new-baked United States specialists in community architecture were busy teaching the people of Ciudad Netzahualcoyotl their problems, needs, and solutions.

The Postprofessional Ethos

The inverse of professionally certified lack, need, and poverty is modern subsistence. The term "subsistence economy" is now generally used only to designate group survival which is marginal to market dependence and in which people make what they use by means of traditional tools and within an inherited, often unexamined, social organization. I propose to recover the term by speaking about modern subsistence. Let us call modern subsistence the style of life that prevails in a postindustrial economy, in which people have succeeded in reducing their market dependence and have done so by protecting—by political means—a social infrastructure in which techniques and tools are used primarily to generate use-values unmeasured and unmeasurable by professional need-makers. I have developed a theory of such tools elsewhere (*Tools for Conviviality*, New York, 1973), and proposed the technical term "convivial tool" for use-value-oriented engineered artifacts. I have shown that the inverse of progressive modernized poverty is a politically generated convivial austerity that protects freedom and equity in the use of such tools.

A retooling of contemporary society with convivial rather than industrial tools implies a shift of emphasis in our struggle for social justice; it implies a new kind of subordination of distributive to participatory justice. In an industrial society, individuals are trained for extreme specialization. They are rendered impotent to shape or to satisfy their own needs. They depend for commodities on the managers who sign the prescriptions for them. The right to the diagnosis of need, the prescription of therapy, and—in general—the distribution of goods predominates in ethics, politics, and law. This emphasis on the right to imputed necessities shrinks to a fragile luxury the liberty to learn or to heal or to move on one's own. In a convivial society, the opposite would be true. The protection of equity in the exercise of personal liberties would be the predominant concern of a society based on radical technology: science and technique at the service of more effective use-value generation. Obviously, such equitably distributed liberty would be meaningless if it were not grounded in the right of equal access to raw materials, tools, and utilities. Food, fuel, fresh air, or living space can no more be equitably distributed than wrenches or jobs, unless they are rationed without regard to imputed need—that is, in equal maximum amounts to young and old, cripple and president. A society dedicated to the protection of equally distributed, modern, and effective tools for the exercise of productive liberties cannot come into existence unless the commodities and resources on which the exercise of these liberties is based are equally distributed to all.

2. Outwitting Developed Nations

This is the text of a lecture addressed in the summer of 1968 to the Kuchiching meeting of the Canadian Foreign Policy Association. I have not revised the text, even where today I would use different language or a different emphasis. It is a reminder of where my thought has evolved from.

It is now common to demand that the rich nations convert their war machine into a program for the development of the Third World. The poorer four-fifths of humanity multiply unchecked while their per capita consumption actually declines. This population expansion and decrease in consumption threatens the industrialized nations, who may still, as a result, convert their defense budgets to the economic pacification of poor nations. And this, in turn, could produce irreversible despair, because the plows of the rich can do as much harm as their swords. United States trucks can do more lasting damage than United States tanks. It is easier to create mass demand for the former than for the latter. Only a minority needs heavy weapons, while a majority can become dependent on unrealistic levels of supply for such productive machines as modern trucks. Once the Third World has become a mass market for the goods, products, and processes which are designed by the rich for themselves, the discrepancy between demand for these Western artifacts and the supply will increase indefinitely. The family car cannot drive the poor into the jet age, nor can a school system provide the poor with education, nor can the family refrigerator ensure healthy food for them.

It is evident that only one man in ten thousand in Latin America can afford a Cadillac, a heart operation, or a Ph.D. This restriction on the goals of development does not make us despair of the fate of the Third World, and the reason is simple. We have not yet come to conceive of a Cadillac as necessary for good transportation, or of a heart operation as normal health care, or of a Ph.D. as the prerequisite of an acceptable education. In fact, we recognize at once that the importation of Cadillacs should be heavily taxed in Peru, that an organ-transplant clinic is a scandalous plaything to justify the concentration of more doctors in Bogota, and that a betatron is beyond the teaching facilities of the University of Sao Paulo.It is not held to be universally evident that the majority of Latin Americans—not only of our generation but also of the next and the next again—cannot afford any kind of automobile, nor any kind of hospitalization, nor for that matter an elementary school education. We suppress our consciousness of this obvious reality because we hate to recognize the corner into which our imagination has been pushed.

So persuasive is the power of the institutions we have created that they shape not only our preferences but actually our sense of possibilities. We have forgotten how to speak about modern transportation that does not rely on automobiles and airplanes. Our conception of modern health care emphasizes our ability to prolong the lives of the desperately ill. We have become unable to think of better education except in terms of more complex schools and of teachers trained for ever longer periods. Huge institutions producing costly services dominate the horizons of our inventiveness.

We have embodied our world-view in our institutions and are now their prisoners. Factories, news media, hospitals, governments, and schools produce goods and services packaged to contain our view of the world. We—the rich—conceive of progress as the expansion of these establishments. We conceive of heightened mobility as luxury and safety packaged by General Motors or Boeing. We conceive of improving the general well-being as increasing the supply of doctors and hospitals, which package health along with protracted suffering. We have come to identify our need for further learning with the demand for ever longer confinement to classrooms. In other words, we have packaged education with custodial care, certification for jobs, and the right to vote, and wrapped them all together with indoctrination in the Christian, liberal, or communist virtues.

In less than a hundred years, industrial society has molded patent solutions to basic human needs and converted us to the belief that man's needs were shaped by the Creator as demands for the products we have invented. This is as true for Russia and Japan as for the North Atlantic community. The consumer is trained for obsolescence, which means continuing loyalty to the same producers, who will give him the same basic packages at a different quality or in new wrappings.

Industrialized societies can provide such packages for personal consumption for most of their citizens, but this is no proof that these societies are sane or economical, or that they promote life. The contrary is true. The more the citizen is trained in the consumption of packaged goods and services, the less effective he seems to become in shaping his environment. His energies and finances are consumed in procuring ever newer models of his staples, and the environment becomes a by-product of his own consumption habits.

The design of the "package deals" of which I speak is the main cause of the high cost of satisfying basic needs. So long as every man "needs" his car, our cities must endure longer traffic jams and absurdly expensive remedies to relieve them. So long as health means maximum length of survival, our sick will get ever more extraordinary surgical interventions and the drugs required to deaden their consequent pain. So long as we want to use school to get children out of their parents' hair or to keep them off the street and out of the labor force, our young will be retained in endless schooling and will need ever increasing incentives to endure the ordeal.

Rich nations now benevolently impose a straitjacket of traffic jams, hospital confinements, and classrooms on the poor nations, and by international agreement call this "development." The rich and schooled and old of the world try to share their dubious blessings by foisting their prepackaged solutions onto the Third World. Traffic jams develop in São Paulo while almost a million northeastern Brazilians flee the drought by walking five hundred miles. Latin American doctors get training at the Hospital for Special Surgery in New York, which they apply to only a few, while amoebic dysentery remains endemic in slums where ninety percent of the population live. A tiny minority get advanced education in basic science in North America—not infrequently paid for by their own governments. If they return at all to Bolivia, they become second-rate teachers of pretentious subjects at La Paz or Cochabamba. The rich export outdated versions of their standard models.

The Alliance for Progress is a good example of benevolent production for underdevelopment. Contrary to its slogans, it did succeed—as an alliance for the progress of the consuming classes, and for the domestication of the Latin American masses. The alliance has been a major step in modernizing the consumption patterns of the middle classes in South America, by integrating them with the dominant culture of the North American metropolis. At the same time, the alliance has modernized the aspirations of the majority of citizens and fixed their demands on unavailable products.

Each car that Brazil puts on the road denies fifty people good transportation by bus. Each merchandised refrigerator reduces the chance of building a community freezer. Every dollar spent in Latin America on doctors and hospitals costs a hundred lives, to adopt a phrase of Jorge de Ahumada, the brilliant Chilean economist. Had each dollar been spent on providing safe drinking water, a hundred lives could have been saved. Each dollar spent on schooling means more privileges for the few at the cost of the many; at best, it increases the number of those who, before dropping out, have been taught that those who stay longer have earned the right to more power, wealth, and prestige. What such schooling does is to teach the schooled the superiority of the better-schooled.

All Latin American countries are frantically intent on expanding their school systems. No country now spends less than the equivalent of eighteen percent of tax-derived public income on education—which means schooling—and many countries spend almost double that. But even with these huge investments, no country has yet succeeded in giving five full years of education to more than one-third of its population; supply and demand for schooling grow geometrically apart. And what is true about schooling is equally true about the products of most institutions in the process of modernization in the Third World.

Continued technological refinements of products which are already established on the market frequently benefit the producer far more than the consumer. The more complex production processes tend to enable only the largest producer to replace outmoded models continually, and to focus the demand of the consumer on the marginal improvement of what he buys, no matter what the concomitant side effects: higher prices, diminished life-spans, less general usefulness, higher costs of repairs. Think of the multiple uses for a simple can opener, whereas an electric one, if it works at all, opens only some kinds of cans, and costs one hundred times as much.

This is equally true for a piece of agricultural machinery and for an academic degree. The Midwestern farmer can become convinced of his need for a four-axle vehicle which can go seventy mph on the highways, has an electric windshield wiper and upholstered seats, and can be turned in for a new one within a year or two. Most of the world's farmers do not need such speed, nor have they ever met with such comfort, nor are they interested in obsolescence. They need low-priced transport, in a world where time is not money, where manual wipers suffice, and where a piece of heavy equipment should outlast a generation. Such a mechanical donkey requires entirely different engineering and design than one produced for the United States market. This vehicle is not in production.

Most of South America needs paramedical workers who can function for indefinite periods without the supervision of an M.D. Instead of establishing a process to train midwives and visiting healers who know how to use a very limited arsenal of medicines while working independently, Latin American universities establish every year a new school of specialized nursing or nursing administration to prepare professionals who can function only in a hospital, and pharmacists who only know how to sell increasingly more dangerous drugs.

The world is reaching an impasse where two processes converge: ever more men have fewer basic choices. The increase in population is widely publicized and creates panic. The decrease in fundamental choice causes anguish and is consistently overlooked. The population explosion overwhelms the imagination, but the progressive atrophy of social imagination is rationalized as an increase of choice between brands. The two processes converge in a dead end: the population explosion provides more consumers for everything from food to contraceptives, while our shrinking imagination can conceive of no other ways of satisfying their demands except through the packages now on sale in the admired societies.

I will focus successively on these two factors, since, in my opinion, they form the two coordinates which together permit us to define underdevelopment.

In most Third World countries, the population grows, and so does the middle class. The income, consumption, and well-being of the middle class are all growing, while the gap between this class and the mass of people widens. Even where per capita consumption is rising, the majority of men have less food now than in 1945, less actual care in sickness, less meaningful work, less protection. This is partly a consequence of polarized consumption and partly caused by the breakdown of the traditional family and culture. More people suffer from hunger, pain, and exposure in 1969 than they did at the end of World War II, not only numerically, but also as a percentage of the world population.

These concrete consequences of underdevelopment are rampant; but underdevelopment is also a state of mind, and understanding it as a state of mind, or as a form of consciousness, is the critical problem. Underdevelopment as a state of mind occurs when mass needs are converted to the demand for new brands of packaged solutions which are forever beyond the reach of the majority. Underdevelopment in this sense is rising rapidly, even in countries where the supply of classrooms, calories, cars, and clinics is also rising. The ruling groups in these countries build up services which have been designed for an affluent culture; once they have monopolized demand in this way, they can never satisfy majority needs.

Underdevelopment as a form of consciousness is an extreme result of what we can call, in the language of both Marx and Freud, *Verdinglichung*, or reification. By reification, I mean the hardening of the perception of real needs into the demand for mass-manufactured products. I mean the translation of thirst into the need for a Coke. This kind of reification occurs in the manipulation of primary human needs by vast bureaucratic organizations which have succeeded in dominating the imagination of potential consumers.

Let me return to my example taken from the field of education. The intense promotion of schooling leads to so close an identification of school attendance and education that in everyday language the two terms are interchangeable. Once the imagination of an entire population has been "schooled," or indoctrinated to believe that school has a monopoly on formal education, then the illiterate can be taxed to provide free high-school and university education for the children of the rich.

Underdevelopment is the result of rising levels of aspiration achieved through the intensive marketing of "patent" products. In this sense, the dynamic underdevelopment that is now taking place is the exact opposite of what I believe education to be: namely, the awakening awareness of new levels of human potential and the use of one's creative powers to foster human life. Underdevelopment, however, implies the surrender of social consciousness to prepackaged solutions.

The process by which the marketing of "foreign" products increases underdevelopment is frequently understood in the most superficial ways. The same man who feels indignation at the sight of a Coca-Cola plant in a Latin American slum often feels pride at the sight of a new normal school growing up alongside. He resents the evidence of a foreign "license" attached to a soft drink which he would like to see replaced by "Cola-Mex." But the same man is willing to impose schooling—at all costs—on his fellow citizens, and is unaware of the invisible license by which this institution is deeply enmeshed in the world market.

Some years ago, I watched workmen putting up a sixty-foot Coca-Cola sign on a desert plain in the Mexquital. A serious drought and famine had just swept over the Mexican highland. My host, a poor Indian in Ixmiquilpan, had just offered his visitors a tiny tequila glass of the costly black sugar-water. When I recall this scene, I still feel anger, but I feel much more incensed when I remember UNESCO meetings at which well-meaning and well-paid bureaucrats seriously discussed Latin American school curricula, and when I think of the speeches of enthusiastic liberals advocating the need for more schools.

The fraud perpetrated by the salesmen of schools is less obvious but much more fundamental than the self-satisfied salesmanship of the Coca-Cola or Ford representative, because the schoolman hooks his people on a much more demanding drug. Elementary-school attendance is not a harmless luxury, but more like the coca chewing of the Andean Indian, which harnesses the worker to the boss.

The higher the dose of schooling an individual has received, the more depressing his experience of withdrawal. The seventh-grade dropout feels his inferiority much more acutely than the dropout from the third grade. The schools of the Third World administer their opium with much more effect than the churches of other epochs. As the mind of a society is progressively schooled, step by step its individuals lose their sense that it might be possible to live without being inferior to others. As the majority shifts from the land into the city, the hereditary inferiority of the peon is replaced by the inferiority of the school dropout, who is held personally responsible for his failure. Schools rationalize the divine origin of social stratification with much more rigor than churches have ever done.

Until this day, no Latin American country has declared youthful underconsumers of Coca-Cola or cars to be lawbreakers, while all Latin American countries have passed laws which define the early dropout as a citizen who has not fulfilled his legal obligations. The Brazilian government recently almost doubled the number of years during which schooling is legally compulsory and free. From now on, any Brazilian dropout under the age of sixteen will be faced during his lifetime with the reproach that he did not take advantage of a legally obligatory privilege. This law was passed in a country where not even the most optimistic could foresee the day when such levels of schooling would be provided for only twenty-five percent of the young. The adoption of international standards of schooling forever condemns most Latin Americans to marginality or exclusion from social life—in a word, underdevelopment.

The translation of social goals into levels of consumption is not limited to only a few countries. Across all frontiers of culture, ideology, and geography today, nations are moving toward the establishment of their own car factories, their own medical and normal schools—and most of these are, at best, poor imitations of foreign and largely North American models.

The Third World is in need of a profound revolution of its institutions. The revolutions of the last generation were overwhelmingly political. A new group of men with a new set of ideological justifications assumed power to administer fundamentally the same scholastic, medical, and market institutions in the interest of a new group of clients. Since the institutions have not radically changed, the new group of clients remains approximately the same size as that previously served. This appears clearly in the case of education. Per pupil costs of schooling are today comparable everywhere, since the standards used to evaluate the quality of schooling tend to be internationally shared. Access to publicly financed education, considered as access to school, everywhere depends on per capita income. (Places like China and North Vietnam might be meaningful exceptions.)

Everywhere in the Third World, modern institutions are grossly unproductive, with respect to the egalitarian purposes for which they are being reproduced. But so long as the social imagination of the majority has not been destroyed by its fixation on these institutions, there is more hope of planning an institutional revolution in the Third World than among the rich. Hence the urgency of the task of developing workable alternatives to "modern" solutions.

Underdevelopment is at the point of becoming chronic in many countries. The revolution of which I speak must begin to take place before this happens. Education again offers a good example: chronic educational underdevelopment occurs when the demand for schooling becomes so widespread that the total concentration of educational resources on the school system becomes a unanimous political demand. At this point, the separation of education from schooling becomes impossible.

The only feasible answer to ever increasing underdevelopment is a response to basic needs that is planned as a long-range goal for areas which will always have a different capital structure. It is easier to speak about alternatives to existing institutions, services, and products than to define them with precision. It is not my purpose either to paint a utopia or to engage in scripting scenarios for an alternate future. We must be satisfied with examples indicating simple directions that research should take.

Some such examples have already been given. Buses are alternatives to a multitude of private cars. Vehicles designed for slow transportation on rough terrain are alternatives to standard trucks. Safe water is an alternative to high-priced surgery. Medical workers are an alternative to doctors and nurses. Community food storage is an alternative to expensive kitchen equipment. Other alternatives could be discussed by the dozen. Why not, for example, consider walking as a long-range alternative to locomotion by machine, and explore the demands which this would impose on the city planner? And why can't the building of shelters be standardized, elements be precast, and each citizen be obliged to learn, in a year of public service, how to construct his own sanitary housing?

It is harder to speak about alternatives in education, partly because schools have recently so completely preempted the available educational resources of good will, imagination, and money. But even here we can indicate the direction in which research must be conducted.

At present, schooling is conceived as graded, curricular class attendance by children, for about one thousand hours yearly, during an uninterrupted succession of years. On the average, Latin American countries can provide each citizen with between eight and thirty months of this service. Why not, instead, make one or two months a year obligatory for all citizens below the age of thirty?

Money is now spent largely on children, but an adult can be taught to read in one-tenth the time and for one-tenth the cost it takes to teach a child. In the case of the adult, there is an immediate return on the investment, whether the main importance of his learning is seen in his new insight, political awareness, and willingness to assume responsibility for his family's size and future, or whether the emphasis is placed on increased productivity. There is a double return in the case of the adult, because he can contribute not only to the education of his children but to that of other adults as well. In spite of these advantages, basic literacy programs have little or no support in Latin America, where schools have a first call on all public resources. Worse, these programs are actually ruthlessly suppressed in Brazil and elsewhere, where military support of the feudal or industrial oligarchy has thrown off its former benevolent disguise.

Another possibility is harder to define, because there is as yet no example to point to. We must therefore imagine the use of public resources for education distributed in such a way as to give every citizen a minimum chance. Education will become a political concern of the majority of voters only when each individual has a precise sense of the educational resources that are owing to him—and some idea of how to sue for them. Something like a universal GI Bill of Rights could be imagined, dividing the public resources assigned to education by the number of children who are legally of school age, and making sure that a child who did not take advantage of his credit at the age of seven, eight, or nine would have the accumulated benefits at his disposal at age ten.

What would the pitiful education credit which a Latin American republic could offer to its children provide? Almost all of the basic supply of books, pictures, blocks, games, and toys that are totally absent from the homes of the really poor, but enable a middle-class child to learn the alphabet, the colors, shapes, and other classes of objects and experiences which ensure his educational progress. The choice between these things and schools is obvious. Unfortunately, the poor, for whom alone the choice is real, never get to exercise this choice.

Defining alternatives to the products and institutions which now preempt the field is difficult, not only, as I have been trying to show, because these products and institutions shape our conception of reality itself, but also because the construction of new possibilities requires a concentration of will and intelligence to a higher degree than ordinarily occurs by chance. This concentration of will and intelligence on the solution of particular problems, regardless of their nature, we have become accustomed over the last century to call research.

I must make clear, however, what kind of research I am talking about. I am not talking about basic research either in physics, engineering, genetics, medicine, or learning. The work of such men as F. H. C. Crick, Jean Piaget, and Murray Gell-Mann may continue to enlarge our horizons in other fields of science. The labs and libraries and specially trained collaborators these men need cause them to congregate in the few research capitals of the world. Their research can provide the basis for new work on practically any product.

I am not speaking here of the billions of dollars annually

spent on applied research, for this money is largely spent by existing institutions on the perfection and marketing of their own products. Applied research is money spent on making planes faster and airports safer; on making medicines more specific and powerful, and on doctors capable of handling their deadly side effects; on packaging more learning into classrooms; on methods for administering large bureaucracies. This is the kind of research for which some kind of counterfoil must somehow be developed if we are to have any chance of coming up with basic alternatives to the automobile, the hospital, and the school, and any of the many other so-called "evidently necessary implements for modern life."

I have in mind a different, and peculiarly difficult, kind of research, which has been largely neglected up to now, for obvious reasons. I am calling for research on alternatives to the products which now dominate the market; to hospitals and the professions dedicated to keeping the sick alive; to schools and the packaging process which refuses education to those who are not of the right age, who have not gone through the right curriculum, who have not sat in a classroom for a sufficient number of successive hours, and who will not pay for their learning with submission to custodial care, screening, and certification, or with indoctrination in the values of the dominant elite.

This counter-research on fundamental alternatives to current prepackaged solutions is the element most critically needed if the poor nations are to have a livable future. Such counter-research is distinct from most of the work done in the name of "the year 2000," because most of that work seeks radical changes in social patterns through adjustments in the organization of an already advanced technology. The counter-research of which I speak must take as one of its assumptions the continued lack of capital in the Third World.

The difficulties of such research are obvious. The researcher must first of all doubt what is obvious to every eye. Second, he must persuade those who have the power of decision to act against their own short-run interests, or bring pressure on them to do so. And finally, he must survive as an individual in a world he is attempting to change fundamentally, so that his fellows among the privileged minority see him as a destroyer of the very ground on which all of us stand. He knows that if he should succeed in the interest of the poor, technologically advanced societies still might envy the "poor" who adopt this vision.

There is a normal course for those who make development policies, whether they live in North or South America, in Russia or Israel. It is to define development and to set its goals in ways with which they are familiar, which they are accustomed to use in order to satisfy their own needs, and which permit them to work through the institutions over which they have power or control. This formula has failed, and must fail. There is not enough money in the world for development to succeed along these lines, not even in the combined arms and space budgets of the superpowers.

An analogous course is followed by those who are trying to make political revolutions, especially in the Third World. Usually, they promise to make the familiar privileges of the present elites, such as schooling and hospital care, accessible to all citizens; they base this vain promise on the belief that a change in political regime will permit them to sufficiently enlarge the institutions that produce these privileges. The promise and appeal of the revolutionary are therefore just as threatened by the counter-research I propose as the market of the now dominant producers.

In Vietnam, a people on bicycles and armed with sharpened bamboo sticks have brought to a standstill the most advanced machinery for research and production ever devised. We must seek survival in a Third World in which human ingenuity can peacefully outwit machined might. The only way to reverse the disastrous trend to increasing underdevelopment, hard as it is, is to learn to laugh at accepted solutions in order to change the demands which make them necessary. Only free men can change their minds and be surprised; and while no men are completely free, some are freer than others.

3. In Lieu of Education

During the late sixties, I conducted a series of seminars at the Centro Intercultural de Documentacion (CIDOC) in Cuernavaca, Mexico, that dealt with the monopoly of the industrial mode of production and with conceptual alternatives that would fit a postindustrial age. The first industrial sector that I analyzed was the school system and its presumed output, education. Seven papers written during this period were published in 1971 under the title Deschooling Society. *From the reactions to that book, I saw that my description of the undesirable latent functions of compulsory schools (the "hidden curriculum" of schooling) was being abused not only by the promoters of so-called "free schools," but even more by schoolmasters who were anxious to transmogrify themselves into adult educators.*

The following essay was written in mid-1971. I here insist that the alternative to the dependence of a society on its schools is not the creation of new devices to make people learn what *experts have decided they need to know; rather, it is the creation of a radically new relationship between human beings and their environment. A society committed to high levels of shared learning and personal intercourse, free yet critical, cannot exist unless it sets pedagogically motivated constraints on its institutional and industrial growth.*

For generations we have tried to make the world a better place by providing more and more schooling, but so far the endeavor has failed. What we have learned instead is that forcing all children to climb an open-ended education ladder cannot enhance equality, but must favor the individual who starts out earlier, healthier, or better prepared; that enforced instruction deadens for most people the will for independent learning; and that knowledge treated as a commodity, delivered in packages, and accepted as private property once it is acquired, must always be scarce.

People have suddenly become aware that public education by means of compulsory schooling has lost its social, its pedagogical, and its economic legitimacy. In response, critics of the educational system are now proposing strong and unorthodox remedies that range from the voucher plan, which would enable each person to buy the education of his choice on an open market, to shifting the responsibility for education from the school to the media and to apprenticeship on the job. Some individuals foresee that the school will have to be disestablished just as the Church was disestablished all over the world during the last two centuries. Other reformers propose to replace the universal school with various new systems that would, they claim, better prepare everybody for life in modern society. These proposals for new educational institutions fall into three broad categories: the reformation of the classroom within the school system; the dispersal of free classrooms throughout society; and the transformation of all society into one huge classroom. But these three approaches—the reformed classroom, the free classroom, and the world-wide classroom—represent three stages in a proposed escalation of education in which each step threatens more subtle and more pervasive social control than the one it replaces.

I believe that the disestablishment of the school has become inevitable, and that this end of an illusion should fill us with hope. But I also believe that the end of the "age of schooling" could usher in the epoch of a global schoolhouse, distinguishable only in name from a global madhouse or a global prison in which education, correction, and adjustment become synonymous. I therefore believe that the breakdown of the school forces us to look beyond its imminent demise and to face fundamental alternatives in education. Either we can work for new and fearsome educational devices that teach about a world which progressively becomes more opaque and forbidding for man, or we can set the conditions for a new era in which technology would be used to make society more simple and transparent, so that all men could once again know the facts and use the tools that shape their lives. In short, we can disestablish schools or we can deschool culture.

The Hidden Curriculum

In order to see clearly the alternatives we face, we must first distinguish learning from schooling, which means separating the humanistic goal of the teacher from the impact of the invariant structure of the school. This hidden structure constitutes a course of instruction that remains forever beyond the control of the teacher or of the school board. It necessarily conveys the message that only through schooling can an individual prepare for adulthood in society, that what is not taught in school is of little value, and that what is learned outside school is not worth knowing. I call it the hidden curriculum because it constitutes the unalterable framework of the schooling system, within which all changes in the visible curriculum are made.

The hidden curriculum is always the same, regardless of school or place. It requires all children of a certain age to assemble in groups of about thirty, under the authority of a certified teacher, for some five hundred or one thousand, or more, hours per year. It does not matter whether the curriculum is designed to teach the principles of fascism, liberalism, Catholicism, socialism, or liberation, so long as the institution claims the authority to define which activities are legitimate "education." It does not matter whether the purpose of the school is to produce Soviet or United States citizens, mechanics, or doctors, so long as you cannot be a legitimate citizen or doctor unless you are a graduate. It makes no difference where the meetings occur—in the auto repair shop, the legislature, or the hospital—so long as they are understood as attendance.

What is important in the hidden curriculum is that students learn that education is valuable when it is acquired in the school through a graded process of consumption; that the degree of success the individual will enjoy in society depends on the amount of learning he consumes; and that learning *about* the world is more valuable than learning *from* the world. The imposition of this hidden curriculum within an educational program distinguishes schooling from other forms of planned education. All the world's school systems have common characteristics, as distinguished from their institutional output, and these are the result of the common hidden curriculum of all schools.

It must be clearly understood that the hidden curriculum translates learning from an activity into a commodity for which the school monopolizes the market. The name we now give to this commodity is "education," a quantifiable and cumulative output of a professionally designed institution called school, whose value can be measured by the duration and the costliness of the application of a process (the hidden curriculum) to the student. The grammar schoolteacher with an M.A. commands a greater salary than one with fewer hours of academic credit, regardless of the relevance of the degree to the task of teaching.

In all "schooled" countries, knowledge is regarded as the first necessity for survival, but also as a form of currency more liquid than rubles or dollars. We have become accustomed, through Karl Marx's writings, to speak of the alienation of the worker from his work in a class society. We must now recognize the estrangement of man from his learning when it becomes the product of a service profession and he becomes the consumer. The more education an individual consumes, the more "knowledge stock" he acquires and the higher he rises in the hierarchy of knowledge capitalists. Education thus defines a new class structure for society within which the large consumers of knowledge—those who have acquired greater quantities of knowledge stock—can claim to be of superior value to society. They represent gilt-edged securities in a society's portfolio of human capital, and access to the more powerful or scarcer tools of production is reserved for them.

The hidden curriculum thus both defines and measures what education is, and to what level of productivity it entitles the consumer. It serves as a rationale for the growing correlation between jobs and corresponding privilege—which translates into personal income in some societies and into direct claims to time-saving services, further education, and prestige in others. (This point is especially important in the light of the lack of correspondence between schooling and occupational competence established in studies such as Ivar Berg's *Education and Jobs: The Great Training Robbery* [New York, 1970].)

The endeavor to put all men through successive stages of enlightenment is rooted deeply in alchemy, the Great Art of the waning Middle Ages. John Amos Comenius (1592–1670), a Moravian bishop, self-styled pansophist, and pedagogue, is rightly considered one of the founders of modern schools. He was among the first to propose seven to twelve grades of compulsory learning. In his *Didactica magna*, he described schools as devices to "teach everybody everything," and outlined a blueprint for an assembly-line production of knowledge, which according to his ideas would make education cheaper and better, and make growth into full humanity possible for all. But Comenius was not only an early efficiency expert; he was an alchemist who adopted the technical language of his craft to describe the art of rearing children. The alchemist sought to refine base elements by conducting their distilled spirits through seven successive stages of sublimation, so that for their own and all the world's benefit they might be transmuted into gold. Of course, the alchemists failed no matter how often they tried, but each time their "science" yielded new reasons for their failure, and they tried again.

Pedagogy opened a new chapter in the history of the *Ars Magna*. Education became the search for an alchemic process that would bring forth a new type of man, who would fit into an environment created by scientific magic. But no matter how much each generation spent on its schools, it always turned out that the majority of people were unfit for enlightenment by this process and had to be discarded as unprepared for life in a man-made world.

Educational reformers who accept the idea that schools have failed fall into three groups. The most respectable are certainly the great masters of alchemy who promise better schools. The most seductive are the popular magicians who promise to make every kitchen into an alchemical laboratory. The most sinister are the new masons of the universe who want to transform the entire world into one huge temple of learning.

Notable among today's masters of alchemy are certain research directors employed or sponsored by the large foundations, who believe that schools, if they could somehow be improved, could also become economically more feasible than those that are now in trouble, and simultaneously could sell a larger package of services. Those who are concerned mainly with the curriculum claim that it is outdated or irrelevant. So, the curriculum is filled with new packaged courses on African Culture, North American Imperialism, Women's Lib, Pollution, or the Consumer Society. Passive learning is wrong—it is, indeed—and so students are graciously allowed to decide what and how they want to be taught. Schools are prison houses; therefore, principals are authorized to approve teachouts, moving the school desks to a roped-off Harlem Street. Sensitivity training becomes fashionable, so we import group therapy into the classroom. School, which was supposed to teach everybody everything, now becomes all things to all children.

Other critics insist that schools make inefficient use of modern science. Some would administer drugs to make it easier for the instructor to change the child's behavior. Others would transform the school into a stadium for educational gaming. Still others would electrify the classroom. If they are simplistic disciples of McLuhan, they replace blackboards and textbooks with multimedia happenings; if they follow Skinner, they claim to be able to modify behavior more efficiently than old-fashioned classroom practitioners.

Most of these changes have, of course, some good effects. The experimental schools have fewer truants. Parents do have a greater feeling of participation in a decentralized district. Pupils assigned by their teacher to an apprenticeship often do turn out more competent than those who stay in the classroom. Some children do improve their knowledge of Spanish in the language lab because they prefer playing with the knobs of a tape recorder to conversing with their Puerto Rican peers. Yet, all these improvements operate within predictably narrow limits, since they leave the hidden curriculum intact.

Some reformers would like to shake loose from the hidden curriculum of public schools, but they rarely succeed. Free schools that lead to further free schools produce a mirage of freedom, even though the chain of attendance is often interrupted by long stretches of loafing. Attendance through seduction inculcates the need for educational treatment more persuasively than reluctant attendance enforced by a truant officer. Permissive teachers in a padded classroom can easily render their pupils impotent to survive once they leave.

Learning in these schools often remains nothing more than the acquisition of socially valued skills, defined, in this instance, by the consensus of a commune rather than by the decree of a school board. New presbyter is but old priest writ large.

Free schools, to be truly free, must meet two conditions: first, they must be run in such a way as to prevent the reintroduction of the hidden curriculum of graded attendance and certified students studying at the feet of certified teachers. And, more important, they must provide a framework in which all participants, staff and pupils, can free themselves from the hidden assumptions of a schooled society. The first condition is frequently stated in the aims of a free school. The second condition is only rarely recognized and is difficult to state as the goal of a free school.

The Hidden Assumptions of Education

It is useful to distinguish between the hidden curriculum, which I have described, and the occult foundations of schooling. The hidden curriculum is a ritual that can be considered the official initiation into modern society, institutionally established through the school. It is the purpose of this ritual to hide from its participants the contradictions between the myth of an egalitarian society and the class-conscious reality it certifies. Once they are recognized as such, rituals lose their power, and this is what is now beginning to happen to schooling. But there are certain fundamental assumptions about growing up—the occult foundations—which now find their expression in the ceremonial of schooling, and which could easily be reinforced by what free schools do.

On first sight, any generalization about free schools seems rash. Especially in the United States, in Canada, and in Germany of 1971, they are the thousand flowers of a new spring. About those experimental enterprises which claim to be *educational institutions*, generalizations can be made. But first we must gain some deeper insight into the relationship between schooling and education.

We often forget that the word "education" is of recent coinage. It was unknown before the Reformation. The education of children is first mentioned in French in a document of 1498. This was the year when Erasmus settled in Oxford, when Savonarola was burned at the stake in Florence, and when Dürer etched his *Apocalypse*, which speaks to us powerfully about the sense of doom hanging over the end of the Middle Ages. In the English language, the word "education" first appeared in 1530—the year when Henry VIII divorced Catherine of Aragon and when the Lutheran Church separated from Rome at the Diet of Augsburg. In Spanish lands, another century passed before the word and idea of education became known. In 1632, Lope de Vega still refers to "education" as a novelty. That year, the University of San Marcos in Lima celebrated its sixtieth anniversary. Learning centers did exist before the term "education" entered common parlance. You "read" the classics or the law; you were not educated for life.

During the sixteenth century, the universal need for "justification" was at the core of theological disputes. It rationalized politics and served as a pretext for large-scale slaughter. The Church split, and it became possible to hold widely divergent opinions of the degree to which all men were born sinful and corrupt and predestined. But by the early seventeenth century, a new consensus began to arise: the idea that man was born incompetent for society and remained so unless he was provided with "education." Education came to mean the inverse of vital competence. It came to mean a process rather than the plain knowledge of the facts and the ability to use tools which shape a man's concrete life. Education came to mean an intangible commodity that had to be produced for the benefit of all and imparted to them in the manner in which the visible Church formerly imparted invisible grace. Justification in the sight of society became the first necessity for a man born in original stupidity, analogous to original sin.

Schooling and education are related to each other like Church and religion, or, in more general terms, like ritual and myth. The ritual created and sustains the myth; it is mythopoeic, and the myth generates the curriculum through which it is perpetuated. "Education," as the designation for an all-embracing category of social justification, is an idea for which we cannot find (outside Christian theology) a specific analogue in other cultures. And the production of education through the process of schooling sets schools apart from other institutions for learning that existed in other epochs. This point must be understood if we want to clarify the shortcomings of most free, unstructured, or independent schools.

To go beyond the simple reform of the classroom, a free school must avoid incorporating the hidden curriculum of schooling which I have described above. An ideal free school tries to provide education and at the same time tries to prevent that education from being used to establish or justify a class structure, from becoming a rationale for measuring the pupil against some abstract scale, and from repressing, controlling, or cutting him down to size. But as long as the free school tries to provide "general education," it cannot move beyond the hidden assumptions of education.

Among these assumptions is what Peter Schrag calls the "immigration syndrome," which impels us to treat all people as if they were newcomers who must go through a naturalization process. Only certified consumers of knowledge are admitted to citizenship. Men are not born equal but are made equal through gestation by Alma Mater. They must be guided away from their natural environment and pass through a social womb in which they are formed to fit sufficiently into everyday life. Free schools often perform this function better than schools of a less seductive kind.

Free educational establishments share with less free establishments another characteristic: they depersonalize the responsibility for education. They place an institution *in loco parentis*. They perpetuate the idea that teaching, if done outside the family, ought to be done by an agency, for which the individual teacher is but an agent. In a schooled society, even the family is reduced to an "agency of acculturation." Educational agencies that employ teachers to perform the corporate intent of their boards are instruments for the depersonalization of intimate relations.

Of course, many free schools do function without accredited teachers. By doing so, they represent a serious threat to the established teachers' unions. But they do not represent a threat to the professional structure of society. A school in which the board appoints people of its own choice to carry out its educational endeavor, even though they hold no professional certificate, license, or union card, is not thereby challenging the legitimacy of the teaching profession any more than a madam, operating in a country which for *legal* operation demands a police license, challenges the social *legitimacy* of the oldest profession by running a private house.

Most teachers who teach in free schools have no opportunity to teach in their own name. They carry out the corporate task of teaching in the name of a board, the less transparent function of teaching in the name of their pupils, or the more mystical function of teaching in the name of "society" at large. The best proof of this is that most teachers in free schools spend even more time than their professional colleagues planning with a committee how the school should educate. When they are faced with the evidence of their illusion, the length of committee meetings drives many generous teachers from public into free school, and, after one year. beyond it.

The rhetoric of all educational establishments states that they form men for something, for the future. But they do not release them for this task before they have developed a high level of tolerance to the ways of their elders: education *for* life rather than *in* everyday life. Few free schools can avoid doing precisely this. Nevertheless, they are among the most important centers from which a new life-style will radiate, not because of the effect their graduates will have, but rather because elders who choose to bring up their children without the benefit of properly ordained teachers frequently belong to a radical minority, and because their preoccupation with the rearing of their children sustains them in their new style.

The Hidden Hand in an Educational Market

The most dangerous category of educational reformers consists of those who maintain that knowledge can be produced and sold much more effectively on an open market than on one controlled by the school. These people argue that skills can be easily acquired from skill models if the learner is truly interested in their acquisition, that individual entitlements can provide a more equal purchasing power for education. They demand a careful separation of the process by which knowledge is measured and certified. These seem to me obvious statements. But it would be a fallacy to believe that the establishment of a free market for knowledge would constitute a radical alternative in education.

The establishment of a free market would indeed abolish what I have previously called the hidden curriculum of present schooling—its age-specific attendance in a graded curriculum. Equally, a free market would at first give the appearance of counteracting what I have called the occult foundations of a schooled society: the "immigration syndrome," the institutional monopoly of teaching, and the ritual of linear initiation. But at the same time, a free market in education would provide the alchemist with innumerable hidden hands to fit each man into the multiple tight little niches that a more complex technocracy can provide.

Many decades of reliance on schooling have turned knowledge into a commodity, a marketable staple of a special kind. Knowledge is now regarded simultaneously as a first necessity and as society's most precious currency. (The transformation of knowledge into a commodity is reflected in a corresponding transformation of language. Words that formerly functioned as verbs are becoming nouns that designate possessions. Until recently, "dwelling" and "learning" and "healing" designated activities. They are now usually conceived as commodities or services to be delivered. We talk about the manufacture of housing or the delivery of medical care; people are no longer regarded as fit to heal or house themselves. In such a society, people come to believe that professional services are more valuable than personal care. Instead of learning how to nurse grandmother, the teenager learns to picket the hospital that does not admit her.) This attitude could easily survive the disestablishment of school, just as affiliation with a church remained a condition for office long after the adoption of the First Amendment. It is even more evident that batteries of tests measuring complex knowledge packages could easily survive the disestablishment of school—and along with them the compulsion to oblige everybody to acquire a minimum package of knowledge stock. The scientific measurement of each person's worth and the alchemistic dream of each person's "educability to his full humanity" would finally coincide. Under the appearance of a free market, the global village would turn into an environmental womb where pedagogic therapists controlled the complex placenta by which each human being was nourished.

At present, schools limit the teacher's competence to the classroom. They prevent him from claiming man's whole life as his domain. The demise of school would remove this restriction and give a semblance of legitimacy to the lifelong pedagogical invasion of everybody's privacy. It would open the way for a scramble for "knowledge" on a free market, which would lead us toward the paradox of a vulgar, albeit seemingly egalitarian, meritocracy.

Schools are by no means the only or the most efficient institutions that pretend to translate information, understanding, and wisdom into behavioral traits, the measurement of which is the key to prestige and power. Nor are schools the first institutions used to convert education into an entitlement. The Chinese mandarin system, for example, was for centuries a stable and effective incentive for education in the service of a relatively open class whose privilege depended on the acquisition of measurable knowledge. Promotion to a scholarly rank did not provide entitlement to any of the coveted jobs, but it did provide a ticket for a public lottery at which offices were distributed by lot among the certified mandarins. No schools, much less universities, developed in China until that country began to wage war with European powers. The testing of independently acquired measurable knowledge enabled the Chinese Empire for three thousand years, alone among nation states in having neither a true church nor a school system, to select its governing elite without establishing a large hereditary aristocracy. Access to this elite was open to the emperor's family and to those who passed tests.

Voltaire and his contemporaries praised the Chinese system of promotion through proven learning. Civil-service testing was introduced in France in 1791, only to be abolished by Napoleon. It would be fascinating to speculate on what would have happened had the mandarin system been chosen to propagate the ideals of the French Revolution, instead of the school system, which inevitably supported nationalism and military discipline. As it happened, Napoleon strengthened the polytechnic, residential school. The Jesuit model of ritual, sequential promotion in a cloistered establishment prevailed over the mandarin system as the preferred method by which Western societies gave legitimacy to their elites.

Principals became the abbots in a world-wide chain of monasteries in which everybody was busy accumulating the knowledge necessary to enter the constantly obsolescent heaven on earth. Just as the Calvinists disestablished monasteries only to turn all of Geneva into one, so we must fear that the disestablishment of school may bring forth a world-wide factory for knowledge. Unless the concept of learning or knowledge is transformed, the disestablishment of school will lead to a wedding between the mandarin system—which separates learning from certification—and a society committed to providing therapy for each man until he be ripe for the gilded age.

The Contradiction of Schools as Tools of Technocratic Progress

Education for a consumer society is equivalent to consumer training. The reform of the classroom, the dispersal of the classroom, and the diffusion of the classroom are different ways of shaping consumers of obsolescent commodities. The survival of a society in which technocracies can constantly redefine human happiness as the consumption of their latest product depends on educational institutions (from schools to ads) that translate education into social control.

In rich countries such as the United States, Canada, or the Soviet Union, huge investments in schooling make the institutional contradictions of technocratic progress very evident. In these countries, the ideological defense of unlimited progress rests on the claim that the equalizing effects of open-ended schooling can counteract the disequalizing force of constant obsolescence. The legitimacy of industrial society itself comes to depend on the credibility of schools, and it does not matter if the GOP or the Communist Party is in power. Under these circumstances, the public is avid for books like Charles Silberman's report to the Carnegie Commission, published as *Crisis in the Classroom* (New York, 1970). Such research inspires confidence because of its well-documented indictment of the present school, in the light of which the insignificant attempts to save the system by manicuring its most obvious faults can create a new wave of futile expectations.

Neither alchemy nor magic nor masonry can solve the problem of the present crisis "in education." The deschooling of our world-view demands that we recognize the illegitimate and religious nature of the educational enterprise itself. Its hubris lies in its attempt to make man a social being as the result of his treatment in an engineered process.

For those who subscribe to the technocratic ethos, whatever is technically possible must be made available at least to a few, whether they want it or not. Neither the privation nor the frustration of the majority counts. If cobalt treatment is possible, then the city of Tegucigalpa must have one apparatus in each of its two major hospitals, at a cost that would free an important part of the population of Honduras from parasites. If supersonic speeds are possible, then some must travel at such speeds. If the flight to Mars can be conceived, then a rationale must be found to make it appear a necessity. In the technocratic ethos, poverty is modernized: not only are old alternatives closed off by new monopolies, but the lack of necessities is also compounded by a growing distance between those services that are technologically feasible and those that are in fact available to the majority.

A teacher turns "educator" when he adopts this technocratic ethos. He then acts as if education were a technological enterprise designed to make man fit into whatever environment the "progress" of science creates. He seems blind to the evidence that constant obsolescence of all commodities comes at a high price: the mounting cost of training people to know about them. He seems to forget that the rising cost of tools is purchased at a high price in education: they decrease the labor-intensiveness of the economy and make learning on the job impossible, or at best the privilege of a few. All over the world, the cost of educating men for society rises faster than the productivity of the entire economy, and fewer people have a sense of intelligent participation in the commonweal.

Further investments in school everywhere render the futility of schooling monumental. Paradoxically, the poor are the first victims of more school. The Wright Commission in Ontario had to report to its government sponsors that post-secondary education is inevitably and without remedy the disproportionate taxing of the poor for an education that will always be enjoyed mainly by the rich.

Experience confirms these warnings. For several decades, a quota system in the Soviet Union favored the admission to the university of sons of working parents over sons of university graduates. Nevertheless, the latter are over-represented in Russian graduating classes much more than they are in those of the United States.

In poor countries, schools rationalize the economic lag of an entire nation. The majority of citizens are excluded from the scarce modern means of production and consumption, but long to enter the economy by way of the school door. The legitimization of hierarchical distribution of privilege and power has shifted from lineage, inheritance, the favor of king or pope, and ruthlessness on the market or on the battlefield to a more subtle form of capitalism: the hierarchical but liberal institution of compulsory schooling, which permits the well-schooled to impute guilt to the lagging consumer of knowledge for holding a certificate of lower denomination. Yet, this rationalization of inequality can never square with the facts, and populist regimes find it increasingly difficult to hide the conflict between rhetoric and reality.

For ten years, Castro's Cuba has devoted great energies to rapid-growth popular education, relying on available manpower, without the usual respect for professional credentials. The initial spectacular successes of this campaign, especially in diminishing illiteracy, have been cited as evidence for the claim that the slow growth rate of other Latin American school systems is due to corruption, militarism, and a capitalist market economy. Yet, the logic of hierarchical schooling is now catching up with Fidel and his attempt to school-produce the New Man. Even when students spend half the year in the cane fields and fully subscribe to the egalitarian ideals of *compañero* Fidel, the school trains every year a crop of self-conscious knowledge consumers ready to move on to new levels of consumption. Also, Dr. Castro faces evidence that the school system will never turn out enough certified technical manpower. Those licensed graduates who do get the new jobs destroy by their conservatism the results obtained by non-certified cadres who muddled into their positions through on-the-job training. Teachers simply cannot be blamed for the failures of a revolutionary government that insists on the institutional capitalization of manpower through a hidden curriculum guaranteed to produce a universal bourgeoisie.

On March 8, 1971, an act of the United States Supreme Court made it possible to begin the legal challenge of the hidden curriculum's legitimacy in that country. Expressing the unanimous opinion of the Court in the case of *Griggs et al. vs. Duke Power Company*, Chief Justice Warren E. Burger stated that "diplomas and tests are useful servants, but Congress has mandated the commonsense proposition that they are not to become masters of reality." The Chief Justice was interpreting the intent of Congress in the equal-opportunities section of the 1964 Civil Rights Act, and the Court was ruling that any school degree or any test given prospective employees must "measure the man for the job" and not the "man in the abstract." The burden of proving that educational requirements are a "reasonable measure of job performance" rests with the employer. In this decision, the Court ruled only on tests and diplomas as means of racial discrimination, but the logic of the Chief Justice's argument applies to any use of an educational pedigree as a prerequisite for employment. Employers will find it difficult to show that schooling is a necessary prerequisite for any job. It is easy to show that it is necessarily antidemocratic because it inevitably discriminates. The Great Training Robbery so effectively exposed by Ivar Berg should now face repeated challenges from students, employers, and taxpayers.

The Recovery of Responsibility for Teaching and Learning

A revolution against those forms of privilege and power that are based on claims to professional knowledge must start with a transformation of consciousness about the nature of learning. This means, above all, a shift of responsibility for teaching and learning. Knowledge can be defined as a commodity only so long as it is viewed as the result of institutional enterprise, or as the fulfillment of institutional objectives. When a man recovers the sense of personal responsibility for what he learns and teaches, this spell can be broken and the alienation of learning from living be overcome.

The recovery of the power to learn or to teach means that the teacher who takes the risk of interfering in somebody else's private affairs also assumes responsibility for the results. Similarly, the student who exposes himself to the influence of a teacher must take responsibility for his own education. For such purposes, educational institutions—if they are needed at all—ideally take the form of facility centers where one can get a roof of the right size over his head and access to a piano or a kiln and to records, books, or slides. Schools, television stations, theaters, and the like are designed primarily for use by professionals. Deschooling society means, above all, the denial of professional status to the second oldest profession, namely, teaching. The certification of teachers now constitutes an undue restriction on the right to free speech; the corporate structure and professional pretensions of journalism an undue restriction on the right to a free press. Compulsory-attendance rules interfere with free assembly. The deschooling of society is nothing less than a cultural mutation by which a people recovers the effective use of its constitutional freedoms: learning and teaching by men who know they are born free rather than treated to freedom. Most people learn most of the time when they do whatever they enjoy; most people are curious and want to give meaning to whatever they come in contact with; and most people are capable of personal, intimate intercourse with others unless they are stupefied by inhuman work or turned off by schooling.

The fact that people in rich countries do not learn much on their own constitutes no proof to the contrary. Rather, it is a consequence of life in an environment from which, paradoxically, they cannot learn much precisely because it is so highly programmed. They are constantly frustrated by the structure of contemporary society, in which the facts that are the basis for making decisions have become more elusive. They live in an environment where tools that can be used for creative purposes have become luxuries, an environment where the channels of communication allow a few to talk to the many.

A New Technology Rather Than a New Education

During the Kennedy years, a peculiar image appeared: knowledge stock. It then gained wide currency in economic thought through Kenneth Boulding. This valuable social good is viewed as the cumulative accretion of the mental excrement of our brightest and best. We here succeed in imagining an anal "capital" that replaces the heaps of earth or gold of previous capitalisms. Instead of bankers and brinksmen, scientists and information storage and retrieval specialists guard it. Meanwhile, thanks to its accruement in a critical mass, it produces interest. A special kind of marketing specialist called an "educator" distributes the stock by channeling it toward those privileged enough to have access to the higher reaches of the international knowledge exchange called "school." Here, these acquire knowledge-holding certificates, which increase the possessor's social value. In some societies, this value translates principally into increased personal income, while in those where knowledge capital is considered too valuable to end up as private property, the value translates into power, rank, and privilege. Such singular treatment is rationalized by the pomp due the guardians of such stock when they put it to further use.

Such a view also affects the manner in which we think of modern technology's development. A contemporary myth would make us believe that the sense of impotence with which most men live today is the consequence of a technology that cannot but create huge systems. But it is not technology that makes systems huge, tools immensely powerful, channels of communication one-directional. Quite the contrary. Properly controlled, technology could provide each man with the ability to understand his environment better and to shape it powerfully with his own hands, and would permit him full intercommunication to a degree never before possible. Such an alternative use of technology constitutes the central alternative in education.

If a person is to grow up, he needs, first of all, access to things, to places, and to processes, to events and to records. He needs to see, to touch, to tinker with, to grasp whatever there is in a meaningful setting. This access is now largely denied. When knowledge became a commodity, it acquired the protections of private property, and thus a principle designed to guard personal intimacy became a rationale for declaring facts off limits for people without proper credentials. In schools, teachers keep knowledge to themselves unless it fits into the day's program. The media inform but exclude those things they regard as unfit to print. Information is locked into special languages, and specialized teachers live off its retranslation. Patents are protected by corporations, secrets are guarded by bureaucracies, and the power to keep others out of private preserves—be they cockpits, law offices, junkyards, or clinics—is jealously guarded by professions, institutions, and nations. Neither the political nor the professional structure of our societies, East and West, could withstand the elimination of the power to keep entire classes of people from facts that could serve them. The access to facts that I advocate goes far beyond truth in labeling. Access must be built into reality, while all we ask of advertising is a guarantee that it does not mislead. Access to reality constitutes a fundamental alternative in education to a system that only purports to teach about it.

Abolishing the right to corporate secrecy—even when professional opinion holds that this secrecy serves the common good—is, as shall presently appear, a much more radical political goal than the traditional demand for public ownership or control of the tools of production. The socialization of tools without the effective socialization of know-how in their use tends to put the knowledge capitalist into the position formerly held by the financier. The technocrat's only claim to power is the stock he holds in some class of scarce and secret knowledge, and the best means to protect its value is a large and capital-intensive organization that renders access to know-how formidable and forbidding.

It does not take much time for the interested learner to acquire almost any skill that he wants to use. We tend to forget this in a society where professional teachers monopolize entrance into all fields and thereby stamp teaching by uncertified individuals as quackery. There are few mechanical skills used in industry or research that are as demanding, complex, and dangerous as driving a car, a skill that most people quickly acquire from a peer. Not all people are suited for advanced logic, yet those who are make rapid progress if they are challenged to play mathematical games at an early age. One out of twenty kids in Cuernavaca can beat me at Whiff 'n' Proof after a couple of weeks' training. In four months, all but a small percentage of motivated adults at our CIDOC center were able to learn Spanish well enough to conduct academic business in the new language.

A first step toward opening up access to skills would be to provide various incentives for skilled individuals to share their knowledge. Inevitably, this would run counter to the interest of guilds and professions and unions. Yet, multiple apprenticeship is attractive; it provides everybody with an opportunity to learn something about almost anything. There is no reason why a person should not combine the abilities to drive a car, repair telephones and toilets, act as a midwife, and function as an architectural draftsman. Special-interest groups and their disciplined consumers would, of course, claim that the public needs the protection of a professional guarantee. But this argument is now steadily being challenged by consumer-protection associations. We have to take much more seriously the objection that economists raise to the radical socialization of skills: that "progress" will be impeded if knowledge—patents, skills, and all the rest—is democratized. Their arguments can be faced only if we demonstrate to them the growth rate of futile diseconomies generated by any existing educational system.

Access to people willing to share their skills is no guarantee of learning. Such access is restricted not only by the monopoly of educational programs over learning and of unions over licensing, but also by a technology of scarcity. The skills that count today are know-how in the use of tools that were designed to be scarce. These tools produce goods or render services that everybody wants but only a few can enjoy, and which only a limited number of people know how to use. Only a few privileged individuals out of the total number of people who have a given disease ever benefit from the results of sophisticated medical technology, and even fewer doctors develop the skill to use them.

The same results of medical research have, however, also been employed to create a basic tool kit that permits army and navy medics, with only a few months' training, to obtain results under battlefield conditions that would have been beyond the expectations of full-fledged doctors during World War II. On an even simpler level, any peasant girl could learn how to diagnose and treat most infections if medical scientists prepared dosages and instructions specifically for a given geographic area.

All these examples illustrate the fact that educational considerations alone suffice to demand a radical reduction of the professional structure that now impedes the relationship between the scientist and the majority of people who want access to science. If this demand were heeded, all men could learn to use yesterday's tools, rendered more effective and durable by modern science, to create tomorrow's world.

Unfortunately, precisely the contrary trend prevails at present. I know a coastal area in South America where most people support themselves by fishing from small boats. The outboard motor is certainly the tool that has changed the lives of these coastal fishermen most dramatically. But in the area I have surveyed, half of all outboard motors that were purchased between 1945 and 1950 are still kept running by constant tinkering, while half of the motors purchased in 1965 no longer run because they were not built to be repaired. Technological progress provides the majority of people with gadgets they cannot afford and deprives them of the simpler tools they need.

The metals, plastics, and ferroconcrete used in building have greatly improved since the 1940s, and ought to provide more people the opportunity to create their own homes. But while in 1948 more than thirty percent of all one-family homes in the United States were owner-built, by the end of the 1960s the percentage of those who acted as their own contractors had dropped to less than twenty percent.

The lowering of the skill level through so-called "economic development" has become even more visible in Latin America. Here, most people still build their own homes from floor to roof. Often they use mud in the form of adobe and thatchwork of unsurpassed utility in the moist, hot, and windy climate. In other places, they make their dwellings out of cardboard, oil drums, and other industrial refuse. Instead of providing people with simple tools and highly standardized, durable, and easily repaired components, all governments have gone in for the mass production of low-cost buildings. It is clear that not one single country can afford to provide satisfactory modern dwelling units for the majority of its people. Yet, everywhere, this policy makes it progressively more difficult for the majority to acquire the knowledge and skills they need to build better houses for themselves.

Self-Chosen "Poverty"

Educational considerations permit us to formulate a second fundamental characteristic that any postindustrial society must possess: a basic tool kit that, by its very nature, counteracts technocratic control. For educational reasons, we must work toward a society in which scientific knowledge is incorporated in tools and components that can be used meaningfully in units small enough to be within the reach of all. Only such tools can socialize access to skills. Only such tools favor temporary associations among those who want to use them on specific occasions. Only such tools allow specific goals to emerge in the process of their use, as any tinkerer knows. Only the combination of guaranteed access to facts and of limited power in most tools renders it possible to envisage a subsistence economy capable of incorporating the fruits of modern science.

The development of such a scientific subsistence economy is unquestionably to the advantage of the overwhelming majority of the people in poor countries. It is also the only alternative to progressive pollution, exploitation, and opaqueness in rich countries. But as we have seen, the dethroning of GNP cannot be achieved without simultaneously subverting GNE—Gross National Education, usually conceived as manpower capitalization. An egalitarian economy cannot exist in a society in which the right to produce is conferred by schools.

The feasibility of a modern subsistence economy does not depend on new scientific inventions. It depends primarily on the ability of a society to agree on fundamental, self-chosen antibureaucratic and antitechnocratic restraints.

These restraints can take many forms, but they will not work unless they touch the basic dimensions of life. (The decision of the United States Congress against development of the supersonic transport plane is one of the most encouraging steps in the right direction.) The substance of these voluntary social restraints would be very simple matters that could be fully understood and judged by any prudent man. (The issues at stake in the SST controversy provide a good example.) All such restraints would be chosen to promote the stable and equal enjoyment of scientific know-how. The French say that it takes a thousand years to educate a peasant to deal with a cow. It would not take two generations to help all people in Latin America or Africa to use and repair outboard motors, simple cars, pumps, medicine kits, and ferroconcrete machines, if their design did not change every few years. And since a joyful life is one of constant meaningful intercourse with others in a meaningful environment, equal enjoyment does translate into equal education.

At present, a consensus on austerity is difficult to imagine. The reason usually given for the impotence of the majority is stated in terms of political or economic class. What is not usually understood is that the new class structure of a schooled society is even more powerfully controlled by vested interests. No doubt an imperialist and capitalist organization of society provides the social structure within which a minority can have disproportionate influence over the effective opinion of the majority. But in a technocratic society, the power of a minority of knowledge capitalists can prevent the formation of true public opinion through control of scientific know-how and the media of communication. Constitutional guarantees of free speech, free press, and free assembly were meant to ensure government by the people. Modern electronics, photo-offset presses, time-sharing computers, and telephones have in principle provided the hardware that could give an entirely new meaning to these freedoms. Unfortunately, these things are used in modern media to increase the power of knowledge bankers to funnel their program-packages through international chains to more people, instead of being used to increase true networks that would provide equal opportunity for encounter among the members of the majority.

Deschooling the culture and social structure requires the use of technology to make participatory politics possible. Only on the basis of a majority coalition can limits to secrecy and growing power be determined without dictatorship. We need a new environment in which growing up can be classless, or we will get a brave new world in which Big Brother educates us all.

4. Tantalizing Needs

This essay reproduces the original text of my Encyclopaedia Britannica *lecture at the University of Edinburgh in early 1974. In this lecture I explored, in the mirror of medicine, what options are left to a community paralyzed in the grip of its tools. By describing the obviously sickening power of the medical system, I drew attention to the paradoxically counterproductive effectiveness of our entirely commodity-centered culture. I developed the theme of this lecture through three successive versions of a book:* Medical Nemesis: The Expropriation of Health *(London, 1974; Paris, 1975; New York, 1976). I present the Edinburgh lecture here in the hope that it will remind the readers of* Medical Nemesis *that the author's purpose in writing on medicine was to illustrate the political and institutional inversion of present-day industrial society at large.*

Within the last decade, the medical establishment has become a major threat to health. The depression, infection, disability, and dysfunction that result from its intervention now cause more suffering than all accidents in traffic and industry. Only the organic damage done by the industrial production of food can rival the ill-health induced by doctors. In addition, medical practice sponsors sickness by the reinforcement of a morbid society which not only industrially preserves its defectives but breeds the therapist's client in a cybernetic way. Finally, the so-called "health professions" have an indirect sickening power, a structurally health-denying effect. They transform pain, illness, and death from a personal challenge into a technical problem, and thereby expropriate the potential of people to deal with their human condition in an autonomous way.

The Backlash of Progress

This ultimate backlash of hygienic progress transcends all technical iatrogenesis; it exceeds the sum of protected malpractice, managerial negligence, and professional callousness against which judicial redress has become increasingly difficult; it is rooted deeper than the maldistribution of resources for which political remedies are still being tried; it is more global than all diseases of medical trial and error. The professional expropriation of health care is the outcome of an unchecked engineering endeavor; it results in the heteronomous maintenance of life on high levels of unhealth, and is experienced as a new kind of horror which I call medical nemesis.

During the last twenty years, the United States price index has risen by about seventy-four percent, but the cost of medical care has escalated by 330 percent. While public expenditure for health care has increased tenfold, out-of-pocket payments for health services have risen threefold and the cost of private insurance eighteenfold. The cost of community hospitals has increased five hundred percent since 1950. The bill for patient care in major hospitals has risen even faster, tripling in eight years. Administrative expenses have multipled by a factor of seven, laboratory costs by a factor of five. Building a hospital bed now costs $65,000, of which two-thirds goes toward mechanical equipment written off or made redundant within ten years or less. Yet, during this same period of unprecedented inflation, life expectancy for adult American males has declined.

The National Health Service in England has had a comparable rate of cost inflation, though it has avoided some of the more astonishing misallocations that fuel public criticism in the United States. Life expectancy in England has not yet declined, but the chronic diseases of middle-aged men have shown an increase, as they did a decade earlier in the United States. In the Soviet Union, physicians and hospital days per capita have tripled over the same period. In China, after a short honeymoon with modern deprofessionalization, the medical-technological establishment has recently grown even faster. The rate at which people become dependent on physicians appears to bear no relation to their form of government. These trends do not represent declining marginal utilities. They are an example of the economics of addiction in which marginal disutilities rise with increasing investment. But, by itself, addiction is not yet nemesis.

In the United States, central-nervous-system agents are the fastest-growing sector of the drug market, making up thirty-one percent of total sales. Over the last twelve years, the rise in per capita consumption for liquor was twenty-three percent, for illegal opiates, about fifty percent, and for prescribed tranquilizers, 290 percent. Some people have tried to explain that this pattern is due to the peculiar way United States physicians receive their lifelong in-service training: in 1970, United States drug companies spent $4,500 in advertising per doctor to reach each of the 350,000 practitioners. Surprisingly, the per capita use of tranquilizers correlates with personal income all over the world, although in many countries the cost of the "scientific education" of the doctor is not included in the price of the drug. But, serious as the rising addiction to doctors and drugs might be, it is only one symptom of nemesis.

Medicine cannot do much for illnesses associated with aging. It cannot cure cardiovascular disease, most cancers, arthritis, multiple sclerosis, or advanced cirrhosis. Some of the pain the aged suffer can sometimes be lessened. Most treatment of the old which requires professional intervention not only heightens their pain but, if it is successful, also protracts it. One is therefore surprised to discover the extent to which resources are spent on the treatment of old age. While ten percent of the United States population is over sixty-five, twenty-eight percent of health-care expenditures are made on behalf of this minority. The old are outgrowing the remainder of the population at a rate of three percent, while the per capita cost of their care is rising at a rate of six percent. Gerontology takes over the GNP. This misallocation of manpower, resources, and social concern will generate unspeakable pain as demands swell and resources dry up. Yet, it too is only a symptom, and nemesis transcends even ritual waste.

Since Nixon and Brezhnev agreed on scientific cooperation in the conquest of space, cancer, and heart disease, coronary-care units have become symbols of peaceful progress and arguments for rising taxes. They require three times the equipment and five times the staff needed for normal patient care; twelve percent of graduate nurses find jobs in such units. They also demonstrate the meaning of professionally conducted embezzlement. Large-scale studies that compare the results of patient care in these units with the home treatment of comparable patients have not yet demonstrated any advantage. The therapeutic value of heart-control stations is probably the same as that of space flights: seen on television, both provide a raindance for millions, who learn to trust science and cease to care for themselves. I happened to be in both Rio de Janeiro and Lima when Dr. Christiaan Barnard was touring there. In both Brazil and Peru, he was able to fill the major football stadium twice in one day, with crowds who hysterically acclaimed his macabre ability to exchange human hearts. Shortly afterwards, I saw well-documented testimonies proving that the Brazilian police have become the first to use life-extension equipment in the torture chamber. Inevitably, when care or healing is transferred to organizations or machines, therapy becomes a death-centered ritual. But nemesis transcends even human sacrifice.

Backfiring Remedies

Prevention of sickness by the intervention of professional third parties has become a fad. Demand for it is growing. Pregnant women, healthy children, workers, or old people are submitted to periodic check-ups and increasingly complex diagnostic procedures. In the process, people are strengthened in their conviction that they are machines whose durability depends on social design. A review of two dozen studies shows that these diagnostic procedures have no impact on mortality and morbidity. In fact, they transform healthy people into anxious patients, and the health risks associated with these attempts at automated diagnosis outweigh any theoretical benefits. Ironically, the serious asymptomatic disorders which this kind of screening alone can discover are frequently incurable illnesses in which early treatment aggravates the patient's morbid condition. But nemesis transcends even terminal torture.

To a point, modern medicine was concerned with therapeutic engineering—the development of strategies for surgical, chemical, or behavioral intervention in the lives of people who are or who might become sick. As it appears that these interventions do not become more effective just because they become more costly, a new level of health engineering has been pushed into the foreground. Health systems are now biased in favor of curative and preventive medicine. New health systems are proposed that are biased in favor of environmental health management. The obsession with immunity gives way to a nightmare of hygiene. As the health-delivery system continually fails to meet the demands made upon it, conditions now classified as illness might well soon be classified as criminal deviance. Imposed medical intervention might be replaced by compulsory re-education or self-criticism. The convergence of individual and environmental hygienic engineering now threatens mankind with a new epidemic in which constantly backfiring countermeasures are absorbed into the plague. This sickening synergy of the technical and nontechnical functions of medicine is what I call hygienic, medical, or tantalizing nemesis.

Industrial Nemesis

Much suffering has always been man-made: history is the record of enslavement and exploitation. It tells of war, and of the pillaging, famine, and pestilence which come in its wake. War between commonwealths and classes has so far been the main planned agency of man-made misery. Thus, man is the only animal whose evolution has been conditioned by adaptation on two fronts. If he did not succumb to the elements, he had to cope with use and abuse by others of his kind. To be capable of this struggle on two frontiers, he replaced instincts by character and culture. A third frontier of possible doom has been recognized since Homer, but common mortals were considered immune to its threat. Nemesis, the Greek name for the doom which threatened from this third direction, was the fate of a few heroes who had fallen prey to the envy of the gods. The common man grew up and perished in a struggle with nature and neighbor. Only the elite would challenge the limits set by nature for man.

Prometheus was not Everyman, but a deviant. Driven by *pleonexia*, or radical greed, he transgressed the boundaries of the human condition. In *hubris*, or measureless presumption, he brought fire from heaven, and thereby brought Nemesis on himself. He was put into irons on a Caucasian rock. An eagle preyed on his liver, and heartlessly healing gods kept him alive by regrafting his liver each night. The encounter with Nemesis made the classical hero an immortal reminder of inescapable cosmic retaliation. He became a subject for epic tragedy, but certainly not a model for everyday aspiration. Now, Nemesis has become endemic; it is the backlash of progress. Paradoxically, it has spread as far and as wide as the franchise, schooling, mechanical acceleration, and medical care. Everyman has fallen prey to the envy of the gods. If the species is to survive, it can do so only by learning to cope on this third frontier.

Most man-made misery is now the by-product of enterprises originally designed to protect the common man in his struggle with the inclemency of the environment and against wanton injustice inflicted by the elite. The main source of pain, disability, and death is now engineered—albeit nonintentional—

harassment. The prevailing ailments, helplessness, and injustice are now the side effects of strategies for progress. Nemesis is now so prevalent that it is readily mistaken for part of the human condition. Common to all previous ethics was the idea that the range of human action was narrowly circumscribed. *Techne* was a measured tribute to necessity and not the road to mankind's chosen action. The desperate disability of contemporary man to envisage an alternative to industrial aggression upon the human condition is an integral part of the curse from which he suffers.

The attempt to reduce nemesis to a political or biological process frustrates any diagnosis of the current institutional crisis. Any study of the so-called "limits-to-growth" controversy becomes futile if it reduces nemesis to a threat which can be met on the the two traditional frontiers. Nemesis does not lose its specific character simply because it has been industrialized. The contemporary crisis of industrial society cannot be understood without distinguishing between the intentionally exploitative aggression of one class against another and the inevitable doom implicit in any disproportionate attempt to transform the human condition. Our predicament cannot be understood without distinguishing between man-made violence and the destructive envy of the cosmos; between the servitude of man to man and the enslavement of man to his gods, which are, of course, his tools. Nemesis cannot be reduced to a problem within the competence of engineers or political managers.

Schooling, transportation, the legal system, modern agriculture, and medicine serve equally well to illustrate how engendered frustration works. Beyond a certain point, the degradation of learning into the result of intentional teaching inevitably compounds a new kind of impotence of the poor majority with a new kind of class structure which discriminates against them. All forms of compulsory, planned learning have these implicit side effects, no matter how much money, good will, political growth, or pedagogic rhetoric is expended in the process; no matter if the world is filled with classrooms or if it is itself transformed into one.

Beyond a certain level of energy, used for the acceleration of any one person in traffic, the transportation industry immobilizes and enslaves the majority of nameless passengers, and provides only questionable marginal advantages to an Olympian elite. No new fuel, technology, or public control can keep the rising mobilization of society from producing increased harriedness, paralysis, and inequity.

Beyond a certain level of capital investment in agriculture and food processing, malnutrition must become pervasive; the green illusion racks the liver of the consumer more effectively than Zeus's eagle. No biological engineering can prevent this result.

Beyond a certain point, the production and delivery of medical care produces more ailments than it can heal. Social security guarantees painful survival more democratically and effectively than the most pitiless gods.

Progress has come with a vengeance which cannot be called a price. The down payment was on the label and can be stated in measurable terms. The compound installments accrue under forms of suffering that exceed the notion of "price." They have led entire societies into a debtors' prison, in which increasing torture for the majority overwhelms and cancels out any possibility of returns that might still benefit the few.

The peasant who switches from weaving his cloth, building his home, and making his tools to the purchase of ready-made clothes, cement beams, and tractors can no longer be satisfied unless he contributes to world-wide nemesis. His neighbor who continues to try to survive on traditional cloth, shelter, and production can no longer live in a world in which industrial nemesis has come to prevail. This double bind is the issue I want to explore. Exasperating greed and blind boldness have ceased to be heroic; they have become part of the social duty of industrialized Everyman. In entering the contemporary market economy, usually by taking the road through schooling, the citizen joins the chorus summoning nemesis. But he also joins a horde of furies unleashed upon those who remain outside the system. The so-called "marginal participants" who do not fully enter into the market economy find themselves deprived of the traditional means of coping with nature and neighbor.

At some point in the expansion of our major institutions, their clients begin to pay a higher price every day for their continued consumption, in spite of evidence that they will inevitably suffer more. At this point in development, the prevalent behavior of society corresponds to that traditionally recognized in addicts. Declining returns pale in comparison with increasing marginal disutilities. *Homo economicus* turns into *Homo religiosus*. His expectations become heroic. The vengeance of economic development not only outweighs the price at which this vengeance was purchased; it also outweighs the compound tort done by nature and neighbor. Classical Nemesis was punishment for the rash abuse of a privilege. Industrialized nemesis is retribution for dutiful participation in society.

War and hunger, pestilence and sudden death, torture and madness, remain man's companions, but they are now shaped into a new *Gestalt* by the nemesis overarching them. The greater the economic progress of any community, the greater the part played by industrial nemesis in the pain, discrimination, and death suffered by its members. Therefore, it seems that the disciplined study of the distinctive character of nemesis ought to be the key theme for research among those concerned with health care, healing, and consoling.

Industrial nemesis is the result of policy formation and decision-making which inevitably produce counterintuitive misadventures. It is the result of a management style which remains a puzzle for the planners. As long as these misadventures are described in the language of science and economics, they remain odd surprises. The language for the study of industrial nemesis must still be forged; it must be capable of describing the contradictions inherent in the thought processes of a society which values operational verification above intuitive evidence.

The Hubris of Tantalus

Medical nemesis is but one aspect of the more general "counterintuitive misadventures" characteristic of industrial society. It is the monstrous outcome of a very specific dream of reason, namely "tantalizing" hubris. Tantalus was a famous king whom the gods invited to Olympus to share one of their meals. He purloined ambrosia, the divine potion that gave the gods unending life. For punishment, he was made immortal in Hades and condemned to suffer unending thirst and hunger. When he bows toward the river in which he stands, the water recedes, and when he reaches for the fruit above his head, the branches move out of his reach. Ethologists might say that hygienic nemesis had programmed him for compulsory counterintuitive behavior.

Craving for ambrosia has now spread to the common mortal. Scientific and political optimism have combined to propagate the addiction. To sustain it, a priesthood of Tantalus has organized itself, offering unlimited medical improvement of human health. The members of this guild pass themselves off as disciples of healing Asklepios, while in fact they peddle ambrosia. People demand of them that life be improved, prolonged, rendered compatible with machines and capable of surviving all modes of acceleration, distortion, and stress. As a result, health has become scarce to the degree that the common man makes health dependent upon the consumption of ambrosia.

Mankind evolved only because each of its individuals came into existence protected by various visible and invisible cocoons. Each one knew the womb from which he had come, and oriented himself by the stars under which he was born. To be human and to become humane, the individual of our species had to find his destiny in his unique struggle with nature and neighbor. He was on his own in the struggle, but the weapons and the rules and the style were given to him by the culture in which he grew up. Cultures evolved, each according to its own viability; and with culture grew people, each learning to stay alive in a common cocoon. Each culture was the sum of rules by which the individual came to terms with pain, sickness, and death, interpreted them, and practiced compassion toward others faced by the same threats. Each culture set up the myths, the rituals, the taboos, and the ethical standards needed to deal with the fragility of life.

Cosmopolitan medical civilization denies the need for man's acceptance of these evils. Medical civilization is planned and organized to kill pain, to eliminate sickness, and to struggle against death. These are new goals, which have never before been guidelines for social life and which are antithetical to every one of the cultures that medical civilization encounters when it is dumped on the so-called "poor" as part and parcel of their economic progress. The health-denying effect of medical civilization is thus equally powerful in rich and in poor countries, even though the latter are often spared some of its more sinister aspects.

The Killing of Pain

For an experience to be pain in the full sense, it must fit into a culture. Precisely because each culture provides a mode for suffering, culture is a particular form of health. The act of suffering is shaped by culture into a question that can be stated and shared.

Medical civilization replaces culturally determined competence in suffering with a growing demand by each individual for the institutional management of his pain. A myriad different feelings, each expressing some kind of fortitude, are homogenized into the political pressure of anesthesia consumers. Pain becomes an item on a list of complaints. As a result, a new kind of horror emerges. Conceptually it is still pain, but the impact on our emotions of this valueless, opaque, and impersonal hurt is something quite new.

In this way, pain has come to pose only a technical question for industrial man: what do I need to set in order to have my pain managed or killed? If the pain continues, the fault is not with the universe, God, my sins, or the devil, but with the medical system. Suffering is an expression of consumer demand for increased medical outputs. By becoming unnecessary, pain has become unbearable. Given this attitude, it now seems rational to flee pain rather than to face it, even at the cost of addiction. It also appears reasonable to eliminate pain, even at the cost of health. It seems enlightened to deny legitimacy to all nontechnical issues that pain raises, even at the cost of disarming the victims of residual pain. For a while, it can be argued that the total amount of pain anesthetized in a society is greater than that of pain newly generated. But at some point, rising marginal disutilities set in. The new suffering is not only unmanageable, but it has lost its referential character. It has become meaningless, questionless torture. Only the recovery of the will and ability to suffer can restore health to pain.

The Elimination of Sickness

Medical interventions have not affected total mortality rates; at best, they have shifted survival from one segment of the population to another. Dramatic changes in the nature of disease afflicting Western societies during the last one hundred years are well documented. First industrialization exacerbated infections, which then subsided. Tuberculosis peaked over a fifty-to-seventy-five-year period and declined before either the tubercle bacillus had been discovered or antituberculosis programs had been initiated. It was replaced in Britain and the United States by major malnutrition syndromes—rickets and pellagra—which peaked and declined and were replaced by diseases of early childhood, which in turn gave way to duodenal ulcer in young men. When that declined, the modern epidemics took their toll: coronary heart disease, hypertension, cancer, arthritis, diabetes, and mental disorders. At least in the United States, death rates from hypertensive heart disease seem to be declining. Despite intensive research, no connection can be demonstrated between these changes in disease patterns and the professional practice of medicine.

The overwhelming majority of modern diagnostic and therapeutic interventions that demonstrably do more good than harm have two characteristics: the material resources for them are extremely cheap, and they can be packaged and designed for self-use or application by family members. The technology that is significantly health-furthering or curative in Canadian medicine costs so little that it could be made available in the entire subcontinent of India for the amount of money now squandered there on modern medicine. On the other hand, the skills needed for the application of the most generally used diagnostic and therapeutic aids are so simple that the careful observation of instructions by people who personally care would guarantee more effective and responsible use than medical practice can provide.

Neither a decline in any of the major epidemics of killing diseases, nor major changes in the age structure of the population, nor falling and rising absenteeism at the workbench, has been significantly related to sick-care or even to immunization. Medical services deserve neither credit for longevity nor blame for the threatening population pressure. Longevity owes much more to the railroad and to the synthesis of fertilizers and insecticides than it owes to new drugs and syringes. Professional practice is both ineffective and increasingly sought out. This technically unwarranted rise in medical prestige can only be explained as a magical ritual for the achievement of goals beyond technical and political reach. It can be countered only through legislation and political action that favor the deprofessionalization of health care.

The professionalization of medicine does not imply and should not be read as implying the negation of specialized healers, of competence, of mutual criticism, or of public control. It does imply a bias against mystification, against the transnational dominance of one orthodox view, against the disbarment of healers chosen by their patients but not certified by the guild. The deprofessionalization of medicine does not mean the denial of public funds for curative purposes; it does mean a bias against the disbursement of any such funds under the prescription and control of guild members rather than under the control of the consumer. Deprofessionalization does not mean the elimination of modern medicine, nor an obstacle to the invention of a new medicine, nor necessarily a return to ancient programs, rituals, and devices. It means that no professional shall have the power to lavish on any one of his patients a package of curative resources larger than that which any other could claim on his own. Finally, the deprofessionalization of medicine does not mean a disregard for the special needs that people manifest at special moments of their lives: when they are born, break a leg, marry, give birth, become crippled, or face death. It only means that people have a right to live in an environment that is hospitable to them at such high points in their experience.

The Struggle Against Death

The ultimate effect of medical nemesis is the expropriation of death. In every society, the image of death is the culturally conditioned anticipation of an uncertain date. This anticipation determines a series of behavioral norms during life and the structure of certain institutions. Wherever modern medical civilization has penetrated a traditional medical culture, a novel cultural ideal of death has been fostered. The new ideal spreads by means of technology and the professional ethos which corresponds to it.

In primitive societies, death is always conceived as the intervention of an actor: an enemy, a witch, an ancestor, or a god. The Christian and the Islamic Middle Ages saw in each death the hand of God. Western death had no face until about 1420. The Western ideal of death which comes to all equally, from natural causes, is of quite recent origin. Only during the autumn of the Middle Ages does death appear as a skeleton with power in its own right. Only during the sixteenth century did European peoples develop the "arte and crafte to knowe ye Will to Dye." For the next three centuries, peasant and noble, priest and whore, prepared themselves throughout life to preside at their own death. Foul death, bitter death, became the end rather than the goal of living. The idea that natural death should come only in healthy old age appeared only in the eighteenth century as a class-specific phenomenon of the bourgeoisie. The demand that doctors struggle against death and keep valetudinarians healthy has nothing to do with their ability to provide such services; Aries has shown that the costly attempts to prolong life appeared at first only among bankers, whose power was compounded by the years they spent at a desk.

We cannot fully understand contemporary social organization unless we see in it a multifaceted exorcism of all forms of evil death. Our major institutions constitute a gigantic defense program waged on behalf of "humanity" against all those people who can be associated with what is currently conceived of as death-dealing social injustice. Not only medical agencies but welfare, international relief, and development programs are enlisted in this struggle. Ideological bureaucracies of all colors join the crusade. Even war has been used to justify the defeat of those who are blamed for wanton tolerance of sickness and death. Producing "natural death" for all men is at the point of becoming an ultimate justification for social control. Under the influence of medical rituals, contemporary death is again the rationale for a witch-hunt.

The Recovery of Health

Rising irreparable damage accompanies present industrial expansion in all sectors. In medicine, these damages appear as iatrogenesis. Iatrogenesis can be direct, as when pain, sickness, and death result from medical care, or it can be indirect, as when health policies reinforce an industrial organization that generates ill-health: it can be structural, when medically sponsored behavior and delusion restrict the vital autonomy of people by undermining their competence in growing up, caring, and aging, or when it nullifies the personal challenge arising from their pain, disability, and anguish.

Most of the remedies proposed for reducing iatrogenesis are engineering interventions, therapeutically designed in their approach to the individual, the group, the institution, or the environment. These so-called "remedies" generate second-order iatrogenic ills by creating a new prejudice against the autonomy of the citizen.

The most profound iatrogenic effects of the medical technostructure result from its nontechnical social functions. The sickening technical and nontechnical consequences of the institutionalization of medicine coalesce to generate a new kind of suffering: anesthetized and solitary survival in a world-wide hospital ward.

Medical nemesis cannot be operationally verified. Much less can it be measured. The intensity with which it is experienced depends on the independence, vitality, and relatedness of each individual. As a theoretical concept, it is one component in a broad theory explaining the anomalies that plague health-care systems in our day. It is a distinct aspect of an even more general phenomenon which I have called industrial nemesis, the backlash of institutionally structured industrial hubris. This hubris consists of a disregard for the boundaries within which the human phenomenon remains viable. Current research is overwhelmingly oriented toward unattainable "breakthroughs." What I have called counterfoil research is the disciplined analysis of the levels at which such reverberations must inevitably damage man.

The perception of enveloping nemesis leads to a social choice. Either the natural boundaries of human endeavor must be estimated, recognized, and translated into politically determined limits, or the alternative to extinction will be compulsory survival in a planned and engineered hell.

In several nations, the public is ready for a review of its health-care system. The frustrations that have become manifest in private-enterprise systems and in socialized care have come to resemble each other frighteningly. The differences between the criticisms by the Russians, French, Americans, and English have become trivial. There is a serious danger that these evaluations will be performed within the coordinates set by post-Cartesian illusions. In rich and in poor countries, the demand for reform of national health care is dominated by demands for equitable access to the wares of the guild, for professional expansion and subprofessionalization, for more truth in the advertising of progress, and for lay control of the temple of Tantalus. The public discussion of the health crisis could easily be used to channel even more power, prestige, and money to biomedical engineers and designers.

There is still time in the next few years to avoid a debate which would reinforce a frustrating system. The coming debate can be reoriented by making hygienic nemesis the central issue. The explanation of nemesis requires simultaneous assessment of both the technical and the nontechnical aspects of medicine, and must focus on it as both industry and religion. The indictment of medicine as a form of institutional hubris exposes precisely those personal illusions that make the critic dependent on health care.

The perception and comprehension of nemesis have, therefore, the power of leading us to policies which could break the magic circle of complaints that now reinforce the dependence of the plaintiff on the health-engineering and planning agencies that he sues. Recognition of nemesis can provide the catharsis to prepare for a nonviolent revolution in our attitudes toward evil and pain. The alternatives to a war against these ills is a search for the peace of the strong.

Health designates a process of adaptation. It is not the result of instinct, but of autonomous and live reaction to an experienced reality. It designates the ability to adapt to changing environments, to growing up and to aging, to healing when damaged, to suffering, and to the peaceful expectation of death. Health embraces the future as well, and therefore includes anguish and the inner resources to live with it.

Man's consciously lived fragility, individuality, and relatedness make the experience of pain, of sickness, and of death an integral part of his life. The ability to cope with this trio autonomously is fundamental to his health. To the degree that he becomes dependent on the management of his intimacy, he renounces his autonomy and his health *must* decline. The true miracle of modern medicine is diabolical. It consists in making not only individuals but whole populations survive on inhumanly low levels of personal health. That health should decline with increasing health-service delivery is unforeseeable only by the health manager, precisely because his strategies are the result of his blindness to the inalienability of health.

The level of public health corresponds to the degree to which the means and responsibility for coping with illness are distributed among the total population. This ability to cope can be enhanced but never replaced by medical intervention in the lives of people or the hygienic characteristics of the environment. That society which reduces professional intervention to the minimum will provide the best conditions for health. The greater the potential for autonomous adaptation to self and to others and to the environment, the less management of adaptation will be needed or tolerated.

The recovery of a healthy attitude toward sickness is neither Luddite nor romantic nor utopian; it is a guiding ideal which will never be fully achieved, which can be achieved with modern devices as never before in history, and which must orient politics to avoid encroaching nemesis.

5. Energy and Equity

"El socialismo puede llegar sólo en bicicleta."
– Jose Antonio Viera-Gallo, Assisant Secretary of Justice in the government of Salvador Allende

This text was first published in Le Monde *in early 1973. Over lunch in Paris, the venerable editor of that daily, as he accepted my manuscript, recommended just one change. He felt that a term as little known and as technical as "energy crisis" had no place in the opening sentence of an article that he would be running on page one. As I now reread the text, I am struck by the speed with which language and issues have shifted in less than five years. But I am equally struck by the slow yet steady pace at which the radical alternative to industrial society—namely, low-energy, convivial modernity—has gained defenders.*

In this essay, I argue that under some circumstances, a technology incorporates the values of the society for which it was invented to such a degree that these values become dominant in every society which applies that technology. The material structure of production devices can thus irremediably incorporate class prejudice. High-energy technology, at least as applied to traffic, provides a clear example. Obviously, this thesis undermines the legitimacy of those professionals who monopolize the operation of such technologies. It is particularly irksome to those individuals within the professions who seek to serve the public by using the rhetoric of class struggle with the aim of replacing the "capitalists" who now control institutional policy by professional peers and laymen who accept professional standards. Mainly under the influence of such "radical" professionals, this thesis has, in only five years, changed from an oddity into a heresy that has provoked a barrage of abuse.

The distinction proposed here, however, is not new. I oppose tools that can be applied in the generation of use-values to others that cannot be used except in the production of commodities. This distinction has recently been re-emphasized by a great variety of social critics. The insistence on the need for a balance between convivial and industrial *tools is, in fact, the common distinctive element in an emerging consensus among groups engaged in radical politics. A superb guide to the bibliography in this field has been published in* Radical Technology *(London and New York, 1976), by the editors of* Undercurrents. *I have transferred my own files on the theme to Valentina Borremans, who is now working on a librarians' guide to reference materials on use-value-oriented modern tools, scheduled for publication in 1978. The specific argument on socially critical energy thresholds in transportation that I pursue in this essay has been elaborated and documented by two colleagues, Jean-Pierre Dupuy and Jean Robert, in their two jointly written books:* La Trahison de l'opulence *(Paris, 1976) and* Les Chronophages *(Paris, 1978).*

The Energy Crisis

It has recently become fashionable to insist on an impending energy crisis. This euphemistic term conceals a contradiction and consecrates an illusion. It masks the contradiction implicit in the joint pursuit of equity and industrial growth. It safeguards the illusion that machine power can indefinitely take the place of manpower. To resolve this contradiction and dispel this illusion, it is urgent to clarify the reality that the language of crisis obscures: high quanta of energy degrade social relations just as inevitably as they destroy the physical milieu.

The advocates of an energy crisis believe in and continue to propagate a peculiar vision of man. According to this notion, man is born into perpetual dependence on slaves, which he must painfully learn to master. If he does not employ prisoners, then he needs machines to do most of his work. According to this doctrine, the well-being of a society can be measured by the number of years its members have gone to school and by the number of energy slaves they have thereby learned to command. This belief is common to the conflicting economic ideologies now in vogue. It is threatened by the obvious inequity, harriedness, and impotence that appear everywhere once the voracious hordes of energy slaves outnumber people by a certain proportion. The energy crisis focuses concern on the scarcity of fodder for these slaves. I prefer to ask whether free men need them.

The energy policies adopted during the current decade will determine the range and character of social relationships a society will be able to enjoy by the year 2000. A low-energy policy allows for a wide choice of life-styles and cultures. If, on the other hand, a society opts for high energy consumption, its social relations must be dictated by technocracy and will be equally degrading whether labeled capitalist or socialist.

At this moment, most societies—especially the poor ones—are still free to set their energy policies by any of three guidelines. Well-being can be identified with high amounts of per capita energy use, with a high efficiency of energy transformation, or with the least possible use of mechanical energy by the most powerful members of society. The first approach would stress the tight management of scarce and destructive fuels on behalf of industry, whereas the second would emphasize the retooling of industry in the interest of thermodynamic thrift. These first two attitudes necessarily imply huge public expenditures and increased social control; both rationalize the emergence of a computerized Leviathan, and both are at present widely discussed.

The possibility of a third option is barely noticed. While people have begun to accept ecological limits on maximum per capita energy use as a condition for physical survival, they do not yet think about the use of minimum feasible power as the foundation of any of various social orders that would be both modern and desirable. Yet, only a ceiling on energy use can lead to social relations that are characterized by high levels of equity. The one option that is at present neglected is the only choice within the reach of all nations. It is also the only strategy by which a political process can be used to set limits on the power of even the most motorized bureaucrat. Participatory democracy postulates low-energy technology. Only participatory democracy creates the conditions for rational technology.

What is generally overlooked is that equity and energy can grow concurrently only to a point. Below a threshold of per capita wattage, motors improve the conditions for social progress. Above this threshold, energy grows at the expense of equity. Further energy affluence then means decreased distribution of control over that energy.

The widespread belief that clean and abundant energy is the panacea for social ills is due to a political fallacy, according to which equity and energy consumption can be indefinitely correlated, at least under some ideal political conditions. Laboring under this illusion, we tend to discount any social limit on the growth of energy consumption. But if ecologists are right to assert that nonmetabolic power pollutes, it is in fact just as inevitable that, beyond a certain threshold, mechanical power corrupts. The threshold of social disintegration by high energy quanta is independent from the threshold at which energy conversion produces physical destruction. Expressed in horsepower, it is undoubtedly lower. This is the fact which must be theoretically recognized before a political issue can be made of the per capita wattage to which a society will limit its members.

Even if nonpolluting power were feasible and abundant, the use of energy on a massive scale acts on society like a drug that is physically harmless but psychically enslaving. A community can choose between Methadone and "cold turkey"—between maintaining its addiction to alien energy and kicking it in painful cramps—but no society can have a population that is hooked on progressively larger numbers of energy slaves and whose members are also autonomously active.

In previous discussions, I have shown that, beyond a certain level of per capita GNP, the cost of social control must rise faster than total output and become the major institutional activity within an economy. Therapy administered by educators, psychiatrists, and social workers must converge with the designs of planners, managers, and salesmen, and complement the services of security agencies, the military, and the police. I now want to indicate one reason why increased affluence requires increased control over people. I argue that, beyond a certain median per capita energy level, the political system and cultural context of any society must decay. Once the critical quantum of per capita energy is surpassed, education for the abstract goals of a bureaucracy must supplant the legal guarantees of personal and concrete initiative. This quantum is the limit of social order.

I will argue here that technocracy must prevail as soon as the ratio of mechanical power to metabolic energy oversteps a definite, identifiable threshold. The order of magnitude within which this threshold lies is largely independent of the level of technology applied, yet its very existence has slipped into the blind-spot of social imagination in both rich and medium-rich countries. Both the United States and Mexico have passed the critical divide. In both countries, further energy inputs increase inequality, inefficiency, and personal impotence. Although one country has a per capita income of $500, and the other one of nearly $5,000, huge vested interest in an industrial infrastructure prods both of them to further escalate the use of energy. As a result, both North American and Mexican ideologues put the label of "energy crisis" on their frustration, and both countries are blinded to the fact that the threat of social breakdown is due neither to a shortage of fuel nor to the wasteful, polluting, and irrational use of available wattage, but to the attempt of industries to gorge society with energy quanta that inevitably degrade, deprive, and frustrate most people.

A people can be just as dangerously overpowered by the wattage of its tools as by the caloric content of its foods, but it is much harder to confess to a national overindulgence in wattage than to a sickening diet. The per capita wattage that is critical for social well-being lies within an order of magnitude which is far above the horsepower known to four-fifths of humanity, and far below the power commanded by any Volkswagen driver. It eludes the underconsumer and the overconsumer alike. Neither is willing to face the facts. For the primitive, the elimination of slavery and drudgery depends on the introduction of appropriate modern technology, and for the rich, the avoidance of an even more horrible degradation depends on the effective recognition of a threshold in energy consumption beyond which technical processes begin to dictate social relations. Calories are both biologically and socially healthy only as long as they stay within the narrow range that separates enough from too much.

The so-called "energy crisis" is, then, a politically ambiguous issue. Public interest in the quantity of power and in the distribution of controls over the use of energy can lead in two opposite directions. On the one hand, questions can be posed that would open the way to political reconstruction by unblocking the search for a postindustrial, labor-intensive, low-energy and high-equity economy. On the other hand, hysterical concern with machine fodder can reinforce the present escalation of capital-intensive institutional growth, and carry us past the last turnoff from a hyperindustrial Armageddon. Political reconstruction presupposes the recognition of the fact that there exist *critical per capita quanta* beyond which energy can no longer be controlled by political process. A universal social straitjacket will be the inevitable outcome of ecological restraints on *total energy use* imposed by industrial-minded planners bent on keeping industrial production at some hypothetical maximum.

Rich countries like the United States, Japan, or France might never reach the point of choking on their own waste, but only because their societies will have already collapsed into a sociocultural energy coma. Countries like India, Burma, and, for another short while at least, China are in the inverse position of being still muscle-powered enough to stop short of an energy stroke. They could choose, right now, to stay within those limits to which the rich will be forced back through a total loss of their freedoms.

The choice of a minimum-energy economy compels the poor to abandon fantastical expectations and the rich to recognize their vested interest as a ghastly liability. Both must reject the fatal image of man the slaveholder currently promoted by an ideologically stimulated hunger for more energy. In countries that were made affluent by industrial development, the energy crisis serves as a pretext for raising the taxes that will be needed to substitute new, more "rational," and socially more deadly industrial processes for those that have been rendered obsolete by inefficient over-expansion. For the leaders of people who are not yet dominated by the same process of industrialization, the energy crisis serves as a *historical imperative* to centralize production, pollution, and their control in a last-ditch effort to catch up with the more highly powered. By exporting their crisis and by preaching the new gospel of puritan energy worship, the rich do even more damage to the poor than they did by selling them the products of now outdated factories. As soon as a poor country accepts the doctrine that more energy more carefully managed will always yield more goods for more people, that country locks itself into the cage of enslavement to maximum industrial outputs. Inevitably, the poor lose the option for rational technology when they choose to modernize their poverty by increasing their dependence on energy. Inevitably, the poor deny themselves the possibility of liberating technology and participatory politics when, together with maximum feasible energy use, they accept maximum feasible social control.

The energy crisis cannot be overwhelmed by more energy inputs. It can only be dissolved, along with the illusion that well-being depends on the number of energy slaves a man has at his command. For this purpose, it is necessary to identify the thresholds beyond which energy corrupts, and to do so by a political process that associates the community in the search for limits. Because this kind of research runs counter to that now done by experts and for institutions, I shall continue to call it counterfoil research. It has three steps. First, the need for limits on the per capita use of energy must be theoretically recognized as a social imperative. Then, the range must be located wherein the critical magnitude might be found. Finally, each community has to identify the levels of inequity, harrying, and operant conditioning that its members are willing to accept in exchange for the satisfaction that comes of idolizing powerful devices and joining in rituals directed by the professionals who control their operation.

The need for political research on socially optimal energy quanta can be clearly and concisely illustrated by an examination of modern traffic. The United States puts between twenty-five and forty-five percent of its total energy (depending upon how one calculates this) into vehicles: to make them, run them, and clear a right of way for them when they roll, when they fly, and when they park. Most of this energy is to move people who have been strapped into place. For the sole purpose of transporting people, two hundred and fifty million Americans allocate more fuel than is used by 1.3 billion Chinese and Indians for all purposes. Almost all of this fuel is burned in a rain-dance of time-consuming acceleration. Poor countries spend less energy per person, but the percentage of total energy devoted to traffic in Mexico or in Peru is probably greater than in the United States, and it benefits a smaller percentage of the population. The size of this enterprise makes it both easy and significant to demonstrate the existence of socially critical energy quanta by the example of personal mobility.

In traffic, energy used over a specific period of time (power) translates into speed. In this case, the critical quantum will appear as a speed limit. Wherever this limit has been passed, the basic pattern of social degradation by high energy quanta has emerged. Once some public utility went faster than fifteen mph, equity declined and the scarcity of both time and space increased. Motorized transportation monopolized traffic and blocked self-powered transit. In every Western country, passenger mileage on all types of conveyance increased by a factor of a hundred within fifty years of building the first railroad. When the ratio of their respective power outputs passed beyond a certain value, mechanical transformers of mineral fuels excluded people from the use of their metabolic energy and forced them to become captive consumers of conveyance. This effect of speed on the autonomy of people is only marginally affected by the technological characteristics of the motorized vehicles employed or by the persons or entities who hold the legal titles to airlines, buses, railroads, or cars. High speed is the critical factor which makes transportation socially destructive. A true choice among practical policies and of desirable social relations is possible only where speed is restrained. Participatory democracy demands low-energy technology, and free people must travel the road to productive social relations at the speed of a bicycle[1].

The Industrialization of Traffic

The discussion of how energy is used to move people requires a formal distinction between transport and transit as the two components of traffic. By *traffic*, I mean any movement of people from one place to another when they are outside their homes. By *transit*, I mean those movements that put human metabolic energy to use, and by *transport*, that mode of movement which relies on other sources of energy. These energy sources will henceforth be mostly motors, since animals compete fiercely with men for their food in an overpopulated world, unless they are thistle eaters like donkeys and camels.

As soon as people become tributaries of transport, not just when they travel for several days, but also on their daily trips, the contradictions between social justice and motorized power, between effective movement and higher speed, between

1 I speak about traffic for the purpose of illustrating the more general point of socially optimal energy use, and I restrict myself to the locomotion of persons, including their personal baggage and the fuel, materials, and equipment used for the vehicle and the road. I purposely abstain from the discussion of two other types of traffic: merchandise and messages. A parallel argument can be made for both, but this would require a different line of reasoning, and I leave it for another occasion. *Author's note:* This note appeared in the original text. I was then preparing two studies that were to complement this text: one on the history of mail delivery, the other on crews and loads throughout history. I renounced both projects to write *Medical Nemesis.*

personal freedom and engineered routing, become poignantly clear. Enforced dependence on auto-mobile machines then denies a community of self-propelled people precisely those values supposedly procured by improved transportation.

People move well on their feet. This primitive means of getting around will, on closer analysis, appear quite effective when compared with the lot of people in modern cities or on industrialized farms. It will appear particularly attractive once it has been understood that modern Americans walk, on average, as many miles as their ancestors—most of them through tunnels, corridors, parking lots, and stores.

People on their feet are more or less equal. People solely dependent on their feet move on the spur of the moment, at three to four mph, in any direction and to any place from which they are not legally or physically barred. An improvement on this native degree of mobility by new transport technology should be expected to safeguard these values and to add some new ones, such as greater range, time economies, comfort, or more opportunities for the disabled. So far, this is not what has happened. Instead, the growth of the transportation industry has everywhere had the reverse effect. From the moment its machines could put more than a certain horsepower behind any one passenger, this industry has reduced equality among men, restricted their mobility to a system of industrially defined routes, and created time scarcity of unprecedented severity. As the speed of their vehicles crosses a threshold, citizens become transportation consumers on the daily loop that brings them back to their home, a circuit which the United States Department of Commerce calls a "trip" as opposed to the "travel" for which Americans leave home equipped with a toothbrush.

More energy fed into the transportation system means that more people move faster over a greater range during the course of every day. Everybody's daily radius expands at the expense of being able to drop in on an acquaintance or walk through the park on the way to work. Extremes of privilege are created at the cost of universal enslavement. An elite packs unlimited distance into a lifetime of pampered travel, while the majority spend a bigger slice of their existence on unwanted trips.

The few mount their magic carpets to travel between distant points that their ephemeral presence renders both scarce and seductive, while the many are compelled to trip farther and faster, and to spend more time preparing for and recovering from their trips.

In the United States, four-fifths of all man-hours on the road are those of commuters and shoppers who hardly ever get into a plane, while four-fifths of the mileage flown to conventions and resorts is covered year after year by the same 1.5 percent of the population, usually those who are either well-to-do or professionally trained to do good. The speedier the vehicle, the larger the subsidy it gets from regressive taxation. Barely 0.2 percent of the entire United States population can engage in self-chosen air travel more than once a year, and few other countries can support a jet-set which is that large.

The captive tripper and the reckless traveler become equally dependent on transport. Neither can do without it. Occasional spurts to Acapulco or to a party congress dupe the ordinary passenger into believing that he has made it into the shrunk world of the powerfully rushed. The occasional chance to spend a few hours strapped into a high-powered seat makes him an accomplice in the distortion of human space, and prompts him to consent to the design of his country's geography around vehicles rather than around people. Man has evolved physically and culturally together with his cosmic niche. What for animals is their environment, he has learned to make into his home. His self-consciousness requires as its complement a life-space and a life-time integrated by the pace at which he moves. If that relationship is determined by the velocity of vehicles rather than by the movement of people, man the architect is reduced to the status of a mere commuter.

The model American male devotes more than 1,600 hours a year to his car. He sits in it while it goes and while it stands idling. He parks it and searches for it. He earns the money to put down on it and to meet the monthly installments. He works to pay for gasoline, tolls, insurance, taxes, and tickets. He spends four of his sixteen waking hours on the road or gathering his resources for it. And this figure does not take into account the time consumed by other activities dictated by transport: time spent in hospitals, traffic courts, and garages; time spent watching automobile commercials or attending consumer-education meetings to improve the quality of the next buy. The model American puts in 1,600 hours to get 7,500 miles: less than five mph. In countries deprived of a transportation industry, people manage to do the same, walking wherever they want to go, and they allocate only three to eight percent of their society's time budget to traffic, instead of twenty-eight percent. What distinguishes the traffic in rich countries from the traffic in poor countries is not more mileage per hour of life-time for the majority, but more hours of compulsory consumption of high doses of energy, packaged and unequally distributed by the transportation industry.

Speed-Stunned Imagination

Past a certain threshold of energy consumption, the transportation industry dictates the configuration of social space. Motorways expand, driving wedges between neighbors and removing fields beyond the distance a farmer can walk. Ambulances take clinics beyond the few miles a sick child can be carried. The doctor will no longer come to the house, because vehicles have made the hospital into the right place to be sick. Once heavy trucks reach a village high in the Andes, part of the local market disappears. Later, when the high school arrives at the plaza along with the paved highway, more and more of the young people move to the city, until not one family is left which does not long for a reunion with someone hundreds of miles away, down on the coast.

Equal speeds have equally distorting effects on the perception of space, time, and personal potency in rich and in poor countries, however different the surface appearances might be. Everywhere, the transportation industry shapes a new kind of man to fit the new geography and the new schedules of its making. The major difference between Guatemala and Kansas is that in Central America some provinces are still exempt from all contact with vehicles and are, therefore, still not degraded by their dependence on them.

The product of the transportation industry is the *habitual passenger*. He has been boosted out of the world in which people still move on their own, and he has lost the sense that he stands at the center of his world. The habitual passenger is conscious of the exasperating time scarcity that results from daily recourse to the cars, trains, buses, subways,and elevators that force him to cover an average of twenty miles each day, frequently criss-crossing his path within a radius of less than five miles. He has been lifted off his feet. No matter if he goes by subway or jet plane, he feels slower and poorer than someone else, and resents the shortcuts taken by the privileged few who can escape the frustrations of traffic. If he is cramped by the timetable of his commuter train, he dreams of a car. If he drives, exhausted by the rush hour, he envies the speed capitalist who drives against the traffic. If he must pay for his car out of his own pocket, he knows full well that the commanders of corporate fleets send the fuel bill to the company and write off the rented car as a business expense. The habitual passenger is caught at the wrong end of growing inequality, time scarcity, and personal impotence, but he can see no way out of this bind except to demand more of the same: more traffic by transport. He stands in wait for technical changes in the design of vehicles, roads, and schedules; or else he expects a revolution to produce mass rapid transport under public control. In neither case does he calculate the price of being hauled into a better future. He forgets that he is the one who will pay the bill, either in fares or in taxes. He overlooks the hidden costs of replacing private cars with equally rapid public transport.

The habitual passenger cannot grasp the folly of traffic based overwhelmingly on transport. His inherited perceptions of space and time, and of personal pace, have been industrially deformed. He has lost the power to conceive of himself outside the passenger role. Addicted to being carried along, he has lost control over the physical, social, and psychic powers that reside in man's feet. The passenger has come to identify territory with the untouchable landscape through which he is rushed. He has become impotent to establish his domain, mark it with his imprint, and assert his sovereignty over it. He has lost confidence in his power to admit others into his presence and to share space consciously with them. He can no longer face the remote by himself. Left on his own, he feels immobile.

The habitual passenger must adopt a new set of beliefs and expectations if he is to feel secure in the strange world where both liaisons and loneliness are products of conveyance. To "gather" for him means to be brought together by vehicles. He comes to believe that political power grows out of the capacity of a transportation system, and its absence is the result of access to the television screen. He takes freedom of movement to be the same as one's claim on propulsion. He believes that the level of democratic process correlates to the power of transportation and communications systems. He has lost faith in the political power of the feet and of the tongue. As a result, what he wants is not more liberty as a citizen, but better service as a client. He does not insist on his freedom to move and to speak to people, but on his claim to be shipped and to be informed by media. He wants a better product rather than freedom from servitude to it. It is vital that he come to see that the acceleration he demands is self-defeating, and that it must result in a further decline of equity, leisure, and autonomy.

Net Transfer of Life-Time

Unchecked speed is expensive, and progressively fewer can afford it. Each increment in the velocity of a vehicle results in an increase in the cost of propulsion and track construction and—most dramatically—in the space the vehicle devours while it is on the move. Past a certain threshold of energy consumption for the fastest passenger, a world-wide class structure of speed capitalists is created. The exchange-value of time becomes dominant, and this is reflected in language: time is spent, saved, invested, wasted, and employed. As societies put price tags on time, equity and vehicular speed correlate inversely.

High speed capitalizes a few people's time at an enormous rate, but, paradoxically, it does this at a high cost in time for all. In Bombay, only a very few people own cars. They can reach a provincial capital in one morning and make the trip once a week. Two generations ago, this would have been a week-long trek once a year. They now spend more time on more trips. But these same few also disrupt, with their cars, the traffic flow of thousands of bicycles and pedicabs that move through downtown Bombay at a rate of effective locomotion that is still superior to that of downtown Paris, London, or New York. The compounded, transport-related time expenditure within a society grows much faster than the time economies made by a few people on their speedy excursions. Traffic grows indefinitely with the availability of high-speed transports. Beyond a critical threshold, the output of the industrial complex established to move people costs a society more time than it saves. The marginal utility of an increment in the speed of a small number of people has for its price the growing marginal disutility of this acceleration for the great majority.

Beyond a critical speed, no one can save time without forcing another to lose it. The man who claims a seat in a faster vehicle insists that his time is worth more than that of the passenger in a slower one. Beyond a certain velocity, passengers become consumers of other people's time, and accelerating vehicles become the means for effecting a net transfer of lifetime. The degree of transfer is measured in quanta of speed. This time-grab despoils those who are left behind, and since they are the majority, it raises ethical issues of a more general nature than the lottery that assigns kidney dialysis or organ transplants.

Beyond a certain speed, motorized vehicles create a remoteness which they alone can shrink. They create distances for all and shrink them for only a few. A new dirt road through the wilderness brings the city within view, but not within reach, of most Brazilian subsistence farmers. The new expressway expands Chicago, but it sucks those who are well-wheeled away from a downtown that decays into a ghetto.

Contrary to what is often claimed, man's speed remained unchanged from the Age of Cyrus to the Age of Steam. News did not travel more than a hundred miles per day, no matter how the message was carried. Neither the Inca's runners nor the Venetian galley, the Persian horseman nor the mail coach on regular runs under Louis XIV broke the barrier. Soldiers, explorers, merchants, and pilgrims moved at twenty miles per day. In Valery's words, Napoleon still had to move at Caesar's slowness: *Napoléon va à la même lenteur que César*. The emperor knew that "public prosperity is measured by the income of the coaches:" *On mesure la prospérité publique aux comptes des diligences*, but he could barely speed them up. Paris–Toulouse had required about two hundred hours in Roman times, and the scheduled stagecoach still took one hundred and fifty-eight hours in 1740, before the opening of the new Royal Roads. Only the nineteenth century accelerated man. By 1830, the trip had been reduced to one hundred and ten hours, but at a new cost. In the same year, 4,150 stagecoaches overturned in France, causing more than a thousand deaths. Then the railroad brought a sudden change. By 1855, Napoleon III claimed to have hit ninety-six kilometers per hour on the train, somewhere between Paris and Marseilles. Within one generation, the average distance traveled each year per Frenchman increased one hundred and thirty times, and Britain's railroad network reached its greatest expansion. Passenger trains attained their optimum cost calculated in terms of time spent for their maintenance and use.

With further acceleration, transportation began to dominate traffic, and speed began to erect a hierarchy of destinations. By now, each set of destinations corresponds to a specific level of speed and defines a certain passenger class. Each circuit of terminal points degrades those pegged at a lower number of miles per hour. Those who must get around on their own power have been redefined as underdeveloped outsiders. Tell me how fast you go and I'll tell you who you are. If you can corner the taxes that fuel the Concorde, you are certainly at the top.

Over the last two generations, the vehicle has become the sign of career achievement, just as the school has become the sign of starting advantage. At each new level, the concentration of power must produce its own kind of rationale. So, for example, the reason that is usually given for spending public money to make a man travel more miles in less time each year is the still greater investment that was made to keep him more years in school. His putative value as a capital-intensive production tool sets the rate at which he is being shipped. Other ideological labels besides "a good education" are just as useful for opening the cabin door to luxuries paid for by others. If the Thought of Chairman Mao must now be rushed around China by jet, this can only mean that two classes are needed to fuel what his revolution has become, one of them living in the geography of the masses and the other in the geography of the cadres. The suppression of intermediary levels of speed in the People's Republic has certainly made the concentration of power more efficient and rational, but it also underscores the new difference in value between the time of the bullock driver and the time of the jet-driven. Acceleration inevitably concentrates horsepower under the seats of a few and compounds the increasing time-lack of most commuters with the further sense that they are lagging behind.

The need for unequal privilege in an industrial society is generally advocated by means of an argument with two sides. The hypocrisy of this argument is clearly betrayed by acceleration. Privilege is accepted as the necessary precondition for improving the lot of a growing total population, or it is advertised as the instrument for raising the standards of a deprived minority. In the long run, accelerating transportation does neither. It only creates a universal demand for motorized conveyance and puts previously unimaginable distances between the various layers of privilege. Beyond a certain point, more energy means less equity.

The Ineffectiveness of Acceleration

It should not be overlooked that top speeds for a few exact a different price than high speeds for all. Social classification by levels of speed enforces a net transfer of power: the poor work and pay to get left behind. But if the middle classes of a speed society may be tempted to ignore discrimination, they should not neglect the rising marginal disutilities of transportation and their own loss of leisure. High speeds for all mean that everybody has less time for himself, as the whole society spends a growing slice of its time budget on moving people. Vehicles running over the critical speed not only tend to impose inequality, they also inevitably establish a self-serving industry that hides an inefficient system of locomotion under apparent technological sophistication. I will argue that a speed limit is not only necessary to safeguard equity; it is equally a condition for increasing the total distance traveled within a society, while simultaneously decreasing the sum total of life-time that transportation claims.

There is little research available on the impact of vehicles on the twenty-four-hour time budget of individuals and societies[2]. From transportation studies, we get statistics on the cost of time per mile, on the value of time measured in dollars or in the length of trips. But these statistics tell us nothing about the hidden costs of transportation: about how traffic nibbles away at life-time, about how vehicles devour space, about the multiplication of trips made necessary by the existence of vehicles, or about the time spent directly and indirectly preparing for locomotion. Further, there is no available measure of the even more deeply buried costs of transport, such as higher rents to live in areas convenient to the flow of traffic, or the cost of protecting these areas from the noise, pollution, and danger to life and limb that vehicles create. The lack of an account of expenditures from the social time budget should not lead us to believe, however, that such an accounting is impossible, nor should it prevent our drawing conclusions from the little that we do know.

From our limited information, it appears that everywhere in the world, after some vehicle broke the speed barrier of fifteen mph, time scarcity related to traffic began to grow. After industry had reached this threshold of per capita output, transport made of man a new kind of waif: a being constantly absent from a destination he cannot reach on his own but must attain within the day. By now, people work a substantial part of every day to earn the money without which they could not even get to work. The time a society spends on transportation grows in proportion to the speed of its fastest public conveyance. Japan now leads the United States in both areas. Life-time gets clut-

2 Since publication of this text in 1973, much research has been done and published. For a critical guide to the literature, see Jean-Pierre Dupuy and Jean Robert, *Les Chronophages* (Paris, 1977).

tered up with activities generated by traffic as soon as vehicles crash through the barrier that guards people from dislocation and space from distortion.

Whether the vehicle that speeds along the public freeway is owned by the state or by an individual has little to do with the time scarcity and overprogramming that rise with every increment in speed. Buses use one-third of the fuel that cars burn to carry one man over a given distance. Commuter trains are up to ten times more efficient than cars. Both could become even more efficient and less polluting. If publicly owned and rationally managed, they could be so scheduled and routed that the privileges they now provide under private ownership and incompetent organization would be considerably cut. But, as long as any system of vehicles imposes itself on the public by top speeds that are not under political control, the public is left to choose between spending more time to pay for more people to be carried from station to station, and paying less taxes so that even fewer people can travel in much less time much farther than others. The order of magnitude of the top speed that is permitted within a transportation system determines the slice of its time budget that an entire society spends on traffic.

The Radical Monopoly of Industry

A desirable ceiling on the velocity of movement cannot be usefully discussed without returning to the distinction between self-powered *transit* and motorized *transport*, and comparing the contribution each component makes relative to the total locomotion of people, which I have called *traffic.*

Transport stands for the capital-intensive mode of traffic, and transit indicates the labor-intensive mode. Transport is the product of an industry whose clients are passengers. It is an industrial commodity and therefore scarce by definition. Improvement of transport always takes place under conditions of scarcity that become more severe as the speed—and with it the cost—of the service increases. Conflict about insufficient transport tends to take the form of a zero-sum game where one wins only if another loses. At best, such a conflict allows for the optimum in the Prisoner's Dilemma: by cooperating with their jailer, both prisoners get off with less time in the cell.

Transit is not the product of an industry, but the independent enterprise of transients. It has use-value by definition, but need not have any exchange-value. The ability to engage in transit is native to man and more or less equally distributed among healthy people of the same age. The exercise of this ability can be restricted by depriving some class of people of the right to take a straight route, or because a population lacks shoes or pavements. Conflict about unsatisfactory transit conditions tends to take, therefore, the form of a non-zero-sum game in which everyone comes out ahead—not only the people who get the right to walk through a formerly walled property, but also those who live along the road.

Total traffic is the result of two profoundly distinct modes of production. These can reinforce each other harmoniously only as long as the autonomous outputs are protected against the encroachment of the industrial product.

The harm done by contemporary traffic is due to the monopoly of transport. The allure of speed has deceived the passenger into accepting the promises made by an industry that produces capital-intensive traffic. He is convinced that high-speed vehicles have allowed him to progress beyond the limited autonomy he enjoyed when moving under his own power. He has allowed planned transport to predominate over the alternative of labor-intensive transit. Destruction of the physical environment is the least noxious effect of this concession. The far more bitter results are the multiplication of psychic frustration, the growing disutilities of continued production, and subjection to an inequitable transfer of power—all of which are manifestations of a distorted relationship between life-time and life-space. The passenger who agrees to live in a world monopolized by transport becomes a harassed, overburdened consumer of distances whose shape and length he can no longer control.

Every society that imposes compulsory speed submerges transit to the profit of transport. Wherever not only privilege but also elementary necessities are denied to those who do not use high-speed conveyances, an involuntary acceleration of personal rhythms is imposed. Industry dominates traffic as soon as daily life comes to depend on motorized trips.

This profound control of the transportation industry over natural mobility constitutes a monopoly much more pervasive than either the commercial monopoly Ford might win over the automobile market, or the political monopoly car manufacturers might wield against the development of trains and buses. Because of its hidden, entrenched, and structuring nature, I call this a *radical monopoly*. Any industry exercises this kind of deep-seated monopoly when it becomes the dominant means of satisfying needs that formerly occasioned a personal response. The compulsory consumption of a high-powered commodity (motorized transport) restricts the conditions for enjoying an abundant use-value (the innate capacity for transit). Traffic serves here as the paradigm of a general economic law: *Any industrial product that comes in per capita quanta beyond a given intensity exercises a radical monopoly over the satisfaction of a need.* Beyond some point, compulsory schooling destroys the environment for learning, medical-delivery systems dry up the nontherapeutic sources of health, and transportation smothers traffic.

Radical monopoly is first established by a rearrangement of society for the benefit of those who have access to the larger quanta; then it is enforced by compelling all to consume the minimum quantum in which the output is currently produced. Compulsory consumption will take on a different appearance in industrial branches where information dominates, such as education or medicine, than it will in those branches where quanta can be measured in British thermal units, such as housing, clothing, or transport. The industrial packaging of values will reach critical intensity at different points with different products, but for each major class of outputs, the threshold occurs within an order of magnitude that is theoretically identifiable. The fact that it is possible theoretically to determine the range of speed within which transportation develops a radical monopoly over traffic does not mean that it is possible theoretically to determine just how much of such a monopoly any given society will tolerate. The fact that it is possible to identify a level of compulsory instruction at which learning by seeing and doing declines does not enable the theorist to identify the specific pedagogical limits to the division of labor that a culture will tolerate. Only recourse to juridical and, above all, to political process can lead to the specific, though provisional, measures by which speed or compulsory education will actually be limited in a given society. The magnitude of voluntary limits is a matter of politics; the encroachment of radical monopoly can be pinpointed by social analysis.

A branch of industry does not impose a radical monopoly on a whole society by the simple fact that it produces scarce products, or by driving competing industries off the market, but rather by virtue of its acquired ability to create and shape the need which it alone can satisfy.

Shoes are scarce all over Latin America, and many people never wear them. They walk on the bare soles of their feet, or wear the world's widest variety of excellent sandals, supplied by a range of artisans. Their transit is in no way restricted by their lack of shoes. But in some countries of South America, people are compelled to be shod ever since access to schools, jobs, and public services was denied to the barefoot. Teachers or party officials define the lack of shoes as a sign of indifference toward "progress." Without any intentional conspiracy between the promoters of national development and the shoe industry, the barefoot in these countries are now barred from any office.

Schools, like shoes, have been scarce at all times. But it was never the small number of privileged pupils that turned the school into an obstacle for learning. Only when laws were enacted to make schools both compulsory and free did the educator assume the power to deny learning opportunities on the job to the underconsumer of educational therapies. Only when school attendance had become obligatory did it become feasible to impose on all a progressively more complex artificial environment into which the unschooled and unprogrammed do not fit.

The potential of a radical monopoly is unmistakable in the case of traffic. Imagine what would happen if the transportation industry could somehow distribute its output more adequately; a traffic utopia of free *rapid* transportation for all would inevitably lead to a further expansion of traffic's domain over human life. What would such a utopia look like? Traffic would be organized exclusively around public-transportation systems. It would be financed by a progressive tax calculated on income and on the proximity of one's residence to the next terminal and to the job. It would be designed so that everybody could occupy any seat on a first-come, first-served basis: the doctor, the vacationer, and the president would not be assigned any priority of person. In this fool's paradise, all passengers would be equal, but they would be just as equally captive consumers of transport. Each citizen of a motorized utopia would be equally deprived of the use of his feet and equally drafted into the servitude of proliferating networks of transportation.

Certain would-be miracle makers, disguised as architects, offer a specious escape from the paradox of speed. By their standards, acceleration imposes inequities, time loss, and controlled schedules only because people do not yet live in those patterns and orbits into which vehicles can best place them. These futuristic architects would house and occupy people in self-sufficient units of towers interconnected by tracks for high-speed capsules. Soleri, Doxiadis, or Fuller would solve the problem created by high-speed transport by identifying the entire human habitat with the problem. Rather than asking how the earth's surface can be preserved for people, they ask how reservations necessary for the survival of people can be established on an earth that has been reshaped for the sake of industrial outputs.

The Elusive Threshold

Paradoxically, the concept of a traffic-optimal top speed for transport seems capricious or fanatical to the confirmed passenger, whereas it looks like the flight of the bird to the donkey driver. Four or six times the speed of a man on foot constitutes a threshold too low to be deemed worthy of consideration by the habitual passenger, and too high to convey the sense of a *limit* to the three-quarters of humanity who still get around on their own power.

All those who plan, finance, or engineer other people's housing, transportation, or education belong to the passenger class. Their claim to power is derived from the value their employers place on acceleration. Social scientists can build a computer model of traffic in Calcutta or Santiago, and engineers can design monorail webs according to abstract notions of traffic flow. Since these planners are true believers in problem-solving by industrial design, the real solution for traffic congestion is beyond their grasp. Their belief in the effectiveness of power blinds them to the disproportionately greater effectiveness of abstaining from its use. Traffic engineers have yet to combine in one simulation model the mobility of people with that of vehicles. The *transportation* engineer cannot conceive of the possibility of renouncing speed and slowing down for the sake of permitting time-and-destination-optimal *traffic* flow. He would never entertain the thought of programming his computer on the stipulation that no motorized vehicle within any city should ever overtake the speed of a velocipede. The development expert who looks down compassionately from his Land-Rover on the Indian peasant herding his pigs to market refuses to acknowledge the relative advantage of feet. The expert tends to forget that this man has dispensed ten others in his village from spending time on the road, whereas the engineer and every member of his family separately devote a major part of every day to transportation. For a man who believes that human mobility must be conceived in terms of indefinite progress, there can be no optimal level of traffic but only passing consensus on a given technical level of transportation.

Most Mexicans, not to speak of Indians and Chinese, are in a position inverse to that of the confirmed passenger. The critical threshold is entirely beyond what all but a few of them know or expect. They still belong to the class of the self-powered. Some of them have a lingering memory of a motorized adventure, but most of them have no personal experience of traveling at or above the critical speed. In the two typical Mexican states of Guerrero and Chiapas, less than one percent of the population moved over ten miles in less than one hour, even once, during 1970. The vehicles into which people in these areas are sometimes crowded render traffic indeed more convenient, but barely faster than the speed of a bicycle. The third-class bus does not separate the farmer from his pig, and it takes them both to market without inflicting any loss of weight, but this acquaintance with motorized "comfort" does not amount to dependence on destructive speed.

The order of magnitude in which the critical threshold of speed can be found is too low to be taken seriously by the passenger, and too high to concern the peasant. It is so obvious it cannot be easily seen. The proposal of a limit to speed within this order of magnitude engenders stubborn opposition. It exposes the addiction of industrialized men to ever higher doses of energy, while it asks those who are still sober to abstain from something they have yet to taste.

To propose counterfoil research is not only a scandal, it is also a threat. Simplicity threatens the expert, who supposedly understands just why the commuter train runs at 8:15 and 8:41, and why it must be better to use fuel with certain additives. That a political process could identify a *natural* dimension, both inescapable and limited, is an idea that lies outside the passenger's world of verities. He has let respect for specialists he does not even know turn into unthinking submission. If a political resolution could be found for problems created by experts in the field of traffic, then perhaps the same remedy could be applied to problems of education, medicine, or urbanization. If the order of magnitude of traffic-optimal vehicular velocities could be determined by laymen actively participating in an ongoing political process, then the foundation on which the framework of every industrial society is built would be shattered. To propose such research is politically subversive. It calls in question the overarching consensus on the need for more transportation which now allows the proponents of public ownership to define themselves as political adversaries of the proponents of private enterprise.

Degrees of Self-Powered Mobility

A century ago, the ball-bearing was invented. It reduced the coefficient of friction by a factor of a thousand. By applying a well-calibrated ball-bearing between two Neolithic millstones, a man could now grind in a day what took his ancestors a week.

The ball-bearing also made possible the bicycle, allowing the wheel—probably the last of the great Neolithic inventions—finally to become useful for self-powered mobility.

Man, unaided by any tool, gets around quite efficiently. He carries one gram of his weight over a kilometer in ten minutes by expending 0.75 calories. Man on his feet is thermodynamically more efficient than any motorized vehicle, and most animals. For his weight, he performs more work in locomotion than rats or oxen, less than horses or sturgeon. At this rate of efficiency, man settled the world and made its history. At this rate, peasant societies spend less than five percent and nomads less than eight percent of their respective social time budgets outside the home or the encampment.

Man on a bicycle can go three or four times faster than the pedestrian, but uses five times less energy in the process. He carries one gram of his weight over a kilometer of flat road at an expense of only 0.15 calories. The bicycle is the perfect transducer to match man's metabolic energy to the impedance of locomotion. Equipped with this tool, man outstrips the efficiency of not only all machines but all other animals as well.

The invention of the ball-bearing, the tangent-spoked wheel, and the pneumatic tire can, taken together, be compared to only three other events in the history of transportation. The invention of the wheel at the dawn of civilization took the load off man's back and put it onto the barrow. The invention and simultaneous application, during the European Middle Ages, of stirrup, shoulder harness, and horseshoe increased the thermodynamic efficiency of the horse by a factor of up to five, and changed the economy of medieval Europe: it made frequent plowing possible and thus introduced rotation agriculture; it brought more distant fields into the reach of the peasant, and thus permitted landowners to move from six-family hamlets into one-hundred-family villages, where they could live around the church, the square, the jail, and—later—the school; it allowed for the cultivation of northern soils and shifted the center of power into cold climates. The building of the first oceangoing vessels by the Portuguese in the fifteenth century, under the aegis of developing European capitalism, laid the solid foundations for a globe-spanning culture and market.

The invention of the ball-bearing signaled a fourth revolution. This revolution was unlike that, supported by the stirrup, which raised the knight onto his horse, and unlike that, supported by the galleon, which enlarged the horizon of the king's captains. The ball-bearing signaled a true crisis, a true political choice. It created an option between more freedom in equity and more speed. The bearing is an equally fundamental ingredient of two new types of locomotion, respectively symbolized by the bicycle and the car. The bicycle lifted man's auto-mobility into a new order, beyond which progress is theoretically not possible. In contrast, the accelerating individual capsule enabled societies to engage in a ritual of progressively paralyzing speed.

The monopoly of a ritual application over a potentially useful device is nothing new. Thousands of years ago, the wheel took the load off the carrier slave, but it did so only on the Eurasian land mass. In Mexico, the wheel was well known, but never applied to transport. It served exclusively for the construction of carriages for toy gods. The taboo on wheelbarrows in America before Cortés is no more puzzling than the taboo on bicycles in modern traffic.

It is by no means necessary that the invention of the ball-bearing continue to serve the increase of energy use and thereby produce time scarcity, space consumption, and class privilege. If the new order of self-powered mobility offered by the bicycle were protected against devaluation, paralysis, and risk to the limbs of the rider, it would be possible to guarantee optimal shared mobility to all people and put an end to the imposition of maximum privilege and exploitation. It would be possible to control the patterns of urbanization if the organization of space were constrained by the power man has to move through it.

Bicycles are not only thermodynamically efficient, they are also cheap. With his much lower salary, the Chinese acquires his durable bicycle in a fraction of the working hours an American devotes to the purchase of his obsolescent car. The cost of public utilities needed to facilitate bicycle traffic versus the price of an infrastructure tailored to high speeds is proportionately even less than the price differential of the vehicles used in the two systems. In the bicycle system, engineered roads are necessary only at certain points of dense traffic, and people who live far from the surfaced path are not thereby automatically isolated as they would be if they depended on cars or trains. The bicycle has extended man's radius without shunting him onto roads he cannot walk. Where he cannot ride his bike, he can usually push it.

The bicycle also uses little space. Eighteen bikes can be parked in the place of one car, thirty of them can move along in the space devoured by a single automobile. It takes three lanes of a given size to move forty thousand people across a bridge in one hour by using automated trains, four to move them on buses, twelve to move them in their cars, and only two lanes for them to pedal across on bicycles. Of all these vehicles, only the bicycle really allows people to go from door to door without walking. The cyclist can reach new destinations of his choice without his tool creating new locations from which he is barred.

Bicycles let people move with greater speed without taking up significant amounts of scarce space, energy, or time. They can spend fewer hours on each mile and still travel more miles in a year. They can get the benefit of technological breakthroughs without putting undue claims on the schedules, energy, or space of others. They become masters of their own movements without blocking those of their fellows. Their new tool creates only those demands which it can also satisfy. Every increase in motorized speed creates new demands on space and time. The use of the bicycle is self-limiting. It allows people to create a new relationship between their life-space and their life-time, between their territory and the pulse of their being, without destroying their inherited balance. The advantages of modern self-powered traffic are obvious, and ignored. That better traffic runs faster is asserted, but never proved. Before they ask people to pay for it, those who propose acceleration should try to display the evidence for their claim.

A grisly contest between bicycles and motors is just coming to an end. In Vietnam, a hyperindustrialized army tried to conquer, but could not overcome, a people organized around bicycle speed. The lesson should be clear. High-energy armies can annihilate people—both those they defend and those against whom they are launched—but they are of very limited use to a people which defends itself. It remains to be seen if the Vietnamese will apply what they learned in war to an economy of peace, if they will be willing to protect the values that made their victory possible. The dismal likelihood is that the victors, for the sake of industrial progress and increased energy consumption, will tend to defeat themselves by destroying that structure of equity, rationality, and autonomy into which American bombers forced them by depriving them of fuels, motors, and roads.

Dominant versus Subsidiary Motors

People are born almost equally mobile. Their natural ability speaks for the personal liberty of each one to go wherever he or she wants. Citizens of a society founded on the notion of equity will demand the protection of this right against any abridgment. It should be irrelevant to them by what means the exercise of personal mobility is denied, whether by imprisonment, bondage to an estate, revocation of a passport, or enclosure within an environment that encroaches on a person's native ability to move in order to make him a consumer of transport. This inalienable right of free movement does not lapse just because most of our contemporaries have strapped themselves into ideological seat belts. Man's natural capacity for transit emerges as the only yardstick by which to measure the contribution transport can make to traffic: there is only so much transport that traffic can bear. It remains to be outlined how we can distinguish those forms of transport that cripple the power to move from those that enhance it.

Transportation can abridge traffic in three ways: by breaking its flow, by creating isolated sets of destinations, and by increasing the loss of time due to traffic. I have already argued that the key to the relation between transport and traffic is the speed of vehicles. I have described how, past a certain threshold of speed, transport has gone on to obstruct traffic in these three ways. It blocks mobility by cluttering up the environment with vehicles and roads. It transforms geography into a pyramid of circuits sealed off from one another according to levels of acceleration. It expropriates life-time at the behest of speed.

If, beyond a certain threshold, transport obstructs traffic, the inverse is also true: below some level of speed, motorized vehicles can complement or improve traffic by permitting people to do things they could not do on foot or on bicycle. A well-developed transportation system running at top speeds of twenty-five mph would have allowed Fix to chase Phileas Fogg around the world in less than half of his eighty days. Motors can be used to transport the sick, the lame, the old, and the just plain lazy. Motor pulleys can lift people over hills, but they can do so peacefully only if they do not push the climber off the path. Trains can extend the range of travel, but can do so with justice only if people have not only equal transportation, but equal free time to come closer to each other. The time engaged in travel must be, as much as possible, the traveler's own: only insofar as motorized transport remains limited to speeds which leave it subsidiary to autonomous transit can a traffic-optimal transportation system be developed.

A limit on the power and therefore on the speed of motors does not, by itself, insure those who are weaker against exploitation by the rich and powerful, who can still devise means to live and work at better located addresses, travel with retinue in plush carriages, and reserve a special lane for doctors and members of the central committee. But at a sufficiently limited maximum speed, this is an unfairness which can be reduced or even corrected by political means: by grassroots control over taxes, routes, vehicles, and their schedules in the community. At unlimited top speed, neither public ownership of the means of transportation nor technical improvements in their control can ever eliminate growing and unequal exploitation. A transportation industry is the key to optimal production of traffic, but only if it does not exercise its radical monopoly over that personal mobility which is intrinsically and primarily a value in use.

Underequipment, Overdevelopmet, and Mature Technology

The combination of transportation and transit that constitutes traffic has provided us with an example of socially optimal per capita wattage, and of the need for politically chosen limits on it. But traffic can also be viewed as but one model for the convergence of world-wide development goals, and as a criterion by which to distinguish those countries that are lamely underequipped from those that are destructively overindustrialized.

A country can be classified as underequipped if it cannot outfit each citizen with a bicycle or provide a five-speed transmission as a bonus for anyone who wants to pedal others around. It is underequipped if it cannot provide good roads for the cycle, or free motorized public transportation (though at bicycle speed!) for those who want to travel for more than a few hours in succession. No technical, economic, or ecological reason exists why such backwardness should be tolerated anywhere in 1975. It would be a scandal if the natural mobility of a people were forced to stagnate on a pre-bicycle level against its will.

A country can be classified as overindustrialized when its social life is dominated by the transportation industry, which has come to determine its class privileges, to accentuate its time scarcity, and to tie its people more tightly to the tracks it has laid out for them.

Beyond underequipment and overindustrialization, there is a place for the world of postindustrial effectiveness, where the industrial mode of production complements other autonomous forms of production. There is a place, in other words, for a world of technological maturity. In terms of traffic, it is the world of those who have tripled the extent of their daily horizon by lifting themselves onto their bicycles. It is just as much the world marked by a variety of subsidiary motors available for the occasions when a bicycle is not enough and when an extra push will limit neither equity nor freedom. And it is, too, the world of the long voyage: a world where every place is open to every person, at his own pleasure and speed, without haste or fear, by means of vehicles that cross distances without breaking with the earth which man walked for hundreds of thousands of years on his own two feet.

Underequipment keeps people frustrated by inefficient labor and invites the enslavement of man by man. Overindustrialization enslaves people to the tools they worship, fattens professional hierarchs on bits and on watts, and invites the translation of unequal power into huge income differentials. It imposes the same net transfers of power on the productive relations of every society, no matter what creed the managers profess, no matter what rain-dance, what penitential ritual, they conduct. Technological maturity permits a society to steer a course equally free of either enslavement. But beware—that course is not charted. Technological maturity permits a variety of political choices and cultures. The variety diminishes, of course, as a community allows industry to grow at the cost of autonomous production. Reasoning alone can offer no precise measure for the level of postindustrial effectiveness and technological maturity appropriate to a concrete society. It can only indicate in dimensional terms the range into which these technological characteristics must fit. It must be left to a historical community engaged in its own political process to decide when programming, space distortion, time scarcity, and inequality cease to be worth its while. Reasoning can identify speed as the critical factor in traffic. Reasoning combined with experimentation can identify the order of magnitude at which vehicular speed turns into a sociopolitical determinant. No genius, no expert, no club of elites can set limits to industrial outputs that will be politically feasible. The need for such limits as an alternative to disaster is the strongest argument in favor of radical technology.

Only when the speed limits of vehicles reflect the enlightened self-interest of a political community can these limits become operative. Obviously, this interest cannot even be expressed in a society where one class monopolizes not only transportation but communication, medicine, education, and weapons as well. It does not matter if this power is held by legal owners or by entrenched managers of an industry that is legally owned by the workers. This power must be reappropriated and submitted to the sound judgment of the common man. The reconquest of power starts with the recognition that expert knowledge blinds the secretive bureaucrat to the obvious way of dissolving the energy crisis, just as it blinded him to the obvious solution to the war in Vietnam.

There are two roads, from where we are, to technological maturity: one is the road of liberation from affluence; the other is the road of liberation from dependence. Both roads have the same destination: the social restructuring of space that offers to each person the constantly renewed experience that the center of the world is where he stands, walks, and lives.

Liberation from affluence begins on the traffic islands where the rich run into one another. The well-sped are tossed from one island to the next and are offered but the company of fellow passengers en route to somewhere else. This solitude of plenty would begin to break down as the traffic islands gradually expanded and people began to recover their native power to move around the place where they lived. Thus, the impoverished environment of the traffic island could embody the beginnings of social reconstruction, and the people who now call themselves rich would break with bondage to overefficient transport on the day they came to treasure the horizon of their traffic islands, now fully grown, and to dread frequent shipments from their homes.

Liberation from dependence starts at the other end. It breaks the constraints of village and valley and leads beyond the boredom of narrow horizons and the stifling oppression of a world closed in on itself. To expand life beyond the radius of tradition without scattering it to the winds of acceleration is a goal that any poor country could achieve within a few years, but it is a goal that will be reached only by those who reject the offer of unchecked industrial development made in the name of an ideology of indefinite energy consumption.

Liberation from the radical monopoly of the transportation industry is possible only through the institution of a political process that demystifies and disestablishes speed and limits traffic-related public expenditures of money, time, and space to the pursuit of equal mutual access. Such a process amounts to public guardianship over a means of production to keep this means from turning into a fetish for the majority and an end for the few. The political process, in turn, will never engage the support of a vast majority unless its goals are set with reference to a standard that can be publicly and operationally verified. The recognition of a socially critical threshold of the energy quantum incorporated in a commodity, such as a passenger-mile, provides such a standard. A society that tolerates the transgression of this threshold inevitably diverts its resources from the production of means that can be shared equitably and transforms them into fuel for a sacrificial flame that victimizes the majority. On the other hand, a society that limits the top speed of its vehicles in accordance with this threshold fulfills a necessary—though by no means sufficient—condition for the political pursuit of equity.

Liberation which comes cheap to the poor will cost the rich dear, but they will pay its price once the acceleration of their transportation systems grinds traffic to a halt. A concrete analysis of traffic betrays the truth underlying the energy crisis: the impact of industrially packaged quanta of energy on the social environment tends to be degrading, exhausting, and enslaving, and these effects come into play even before those which threaten the pollution of the physical environment and the extinction of the race. The crucial point at which these effects can be reversed is not, however, a matter of deduction, but of decision.

About the Author

Ivan Illich was born in 1926 in Vienna, Austria, and grew up in Europe. After studies in the natural sciences, he obtained degrees in history, philosophy, and theology. In 1950, he came to New York, where he worked for five years as a parish priest in an Irish-Puerto Rican neighborhood. The following five years, he lived in Puerto Rico. Since 1960, he has made his home in Cuernavaca, Mexico. Illich is the author of *Celebration of Awareness* (1969), *Deschooling Society* (1971), *Tools of Conviviality* (1973), *Energy and Equity* (1974), and *Medical Nemesis* (1976).

www.ingramcontent.com/pod-product-compliance
Ingram Content Group UK Ltd.
Pitfield, Milton Keynes, MK11 3LW, UK
UKHW061504190826
474231UK00001B/9

9 781800 508705